Prohibition

Other books in the History Firsthand series:

HISTORY
FIRSTHAND

Prohibition

Dennis Nishi, *Book Editor*

Daniel Leone, *President*
Bonnie Szumski, *Publisher*
Scott Barbour, *Managing Editor*
David M. Haugen, *Series Editor*

GREENHAVEN
PRESS®

THOMSON
━━━━✳━━━━ ™
GALE

San Diego • Detroit • New York • San Francisco • Cleveland
New Haven, Conn. • Waterville, Maine • London • Munich

363.4
Pro

THOMSON

GALE

LIBRARY OF CONGRESS CATALOGING-IN-PUBLICATION DATA
Prohibition / by Dennis Nishi, book editor.
p. cm. — (History firsthand)
Includes bibliographical references and index.
ISBN 0-7377-1306-2 (hardback : alk. paper) —
ISBN 0-7377-1307-0 (pbk. : alk. paper)
1. Prohibition—United States—History. I. Nishi, Dennis, 1967– II. Series.
HV5089 .P748   2003
363.4'1'0973—dc21   2002001267

Printed in the United States of America

Contents

Chapter 2: The Wets

Chapter Preface

1. Prohibition Is the Devil's Deceit
by Joseph F. Rutherford
Judge Rutherford was the second president of the Watchtower Society. The Watchtower Society was one of the few Christian organizations that fought against Prohibition.

2. The Puritanical Foundations of the Prohibition Movement
by Clarence Darrow
Attorney Clarence Darrow describes the origin of Prohibition as well as other restrictions imposed by religious organizations throughout U.S. history.

3. Prohibition Is Contrary to Human Nature
by Percy Andreae
Andreae was a lobbyist sponsored by the liquor industry. He criticizes the prohibitionists' zeal to control human nature.

4. Prohibition Is Unenforceable
by Fiorello H. La Guardia
Congressman and future mayor of New York La Guardia testifies before the Senate about the impossibility of enforcing Prohibition.

Chapter 3: The Cops and the Criminals

Chapter Preface

1. Prohibition Agent No. 1
by Izzy Einstein
Einstein used unconventional methods to root out speakeasies and other businesses that continued to serve alcohol during Prohibition. In an excerpt from Einstein's autobiography, he describes some of his successful raids.

2. The Danger of Unfit Prohibition Agents
by Mabel Walker Willebrandt
Willebrandt formerly held the position of assistant U.S. attorney general in charge of Prohibition cases.

Chapter 5: Repeal

rebutal

5. Prohibition Was a Success

Foreword

I n his preface to a book on the events leading to the Civil War, Stephen B. Oates, the historian and biographer of Abraham Lincoln, John Brown, and other noteworthy American historical figures, explained the difficulty of writing history in the traditional third-person voice of the biographer and historian. "The trouble, I realized, was the detached third-person voice," wrote Oates. "It seemed to wring all the life out of my characters and the antebellum era." Indeed, how can a historian, even one as prominent as Oates, compete with the eloquent voices of Daniel Webster, Abraham Lincoln, Harriet Beecher Stowe, Frederick Douglass, and Robert E. Lee?

Oates's comment notwithstanding, every student of history, professional and amateur alike, can name a score of excellent accounts written in the traditional third-person voice of the historian that bring to life an event or an era and the people who lived through it. In *Battle Cry of Freedom*, James M. McPherson vividly re-creates the American Civil War. Barbara Tuchman's *The Guns of August* captures in sharp detail the tensions in Europe that led to the outbreak of World War I. Taylor Branch's *Parting the Waters* provides a detailed and dramatic account of the American Civil Rights Movement. The study of history would be impossible without such guiding texts.

Nonetheless, Oates's comment makes a compelling point. Often the most convincing tellers of history are those who lived through the event, the eyewitnesses who recorded their firsthand experiences in autobiographies, speeches, memoirs, journals, and letters. The Greenhaven Press History Firsthand series presents history through the words of first-person narrators. Each text in this series captures a significant historical era or event—the American Civil War, the

Great Depression, the Holocaust, the Roaring Twenties, the 1960s, the Vietnam War. Readers will investigate these historical eras and events by examining primary-source documents, authored by chroniclers both famous and little known. The texts in the History Firsthand series comprise the celebrated and familiar words of the presidents, generals, and famous men and women of letters who recorded their impressions for posterity, as well as the statements of the ordinary people who struggled to understand the storm of events around them—the foot soldiers who fought the great battles and their loved ones back home, the men and women who waited on the breadlines, the college students who marched in protest.

The texts in this series are particularly suited to students beginning serious historical study. By examining these firsthand documents, novice historians can begin to form their own insights and conclusions about the historical era or event under investigation. To aid the student in that process, the texts in the History Firsthand series include introductions that provide an overview of the era or event, timelines, and bibliographies that point the serious student toward key historical works for further study.

The study of history commences with an examination of words—the testimony of witnesses who lived through an era or event and left for future generations the task of making sense of their accounts. The Greenhaven Press History Firsthand series invites the beginner historian to commence the process of historical investigation by focusing on the words of those individuals who made history by living through it and recording their experiences firsthand.

Introduction: The Noble Experiment

The Eighteenth Amendment to the Constitution, which imposed national prohibition, took effect on January 16, 1920. The measure sought to eliminate alcohol usage in America by outlawing the sale, manufacture, and transportation of alcohol in the United States. It was a seemingly victorious conclusion to a fifty-year battle for temperance (the reduction or abstinence from alcohol). But the "noble experiment," as President Hoover called Prohibition, had many fatal shortcomings. One of the biggest mistakes lawmakers made was underestimating the willingness of the general public to break the law. Although Prohibition gave a boost to bootlegging, rum-running, and organized crime, it was the patronage of ordinary citizens which kept the estimated thirty thousand speakeasies (illegal bars) in New York alone in business. Many critics of Prohibition, including New York politician Fiorello La Guardia, argued that the flagrant disregard for Prohibition laws could undermine the entire legal system of the nation. After all, if people could dismiss any law they did not believe in how could order ever be maintained? Fortunately, most Americans limited their civil disobedience to drinking—a tradition which, history shows, Americans were not willing to give up despite the optimistic and generally moralistic goals of Prohibition advocates.

The Roots of Prohibition

Prohibition of alcohol in 1920 would last over thirteen years, making it the longest ban on alcohol in U.S. history. But it was not the first successful temperance campaign on record. The first prohibition in America can be traced all the way back to colonial times. In 1733, British general James

Oglethorpe was determined to create a sober society free of alcohol. Unfortunately, his efforts to keep the colony of Georgia dry were thwarted by bootleggers from the Carolinas and uncooperative colonists who ignored the law. The edict was rescinded in 1742 and would foreshadow events to come.

As alcohol usage continued in the young nation, temperance societies were formed in response to the abuses and ill effects of drinking. These organizations were made up of people who made voluntary pledges of temperance. Typically founded by churchgoers—especially Christian women—who saw the excess of alcohol use as sinful, temperance societies initially urged moderation. But over time they came to believe the addictive qualities of alcohol were too corrupting of an influence in any quantity. Temperance advocates pushed for total abstinence, including beer, wine, and ciders. One of the pioneer temperance organizations, the American Temperance Society, was founded in 1826. They marked the names of completely "dry" members in their roles with the letter "T" for "total" abstinence. The word "teetotaler" derives this now antiquated temperance term.

The movement spread until a temperance society could be found in every state. Buoyed by their growing membership, temperance leaders took the movement to the next level and often successfully lobbied for local prohibition laws. When the Supreme Court gave states the power to regulate the sale of alcohol in 1847, temperance groups seized the opportunity to push for laws at the state level. Within the next few years, a dozen states, led by Maine, passed statewide prohibitions. But the laws did not stand long. One by one, every state except Maine repealed their laws. One of the reasons was the growing threat of the Civil War. Americans lost interest in the smaller issues like temperance, and dry leaders, who were usually active abolitionists as well, turned their full attention to the slavery issue. In addition, President Lincoln signed the Internal Revenue Act in 1862, which placed a fee on all liquor sold in Union states to raise money for the war effort. This was a blow to the prohibition movement as it essentially gave drinking of alcohol government approval and, ironically, a patriotic dimension.

The Temperance Movement Gathers Steam

The nation changed dramatically after the Civil War. The population grew rapidly and the landscape became more urbanized. Large numbers of people in the country abandoned their agricultural roots to move into cities where rapid industrialization offered jobs. There they found life to be different and oftentimes harsh. Drinking increased substantially among the working class. Long work hours for little pay drove them to seek retreat in friendly saloons that seemed to spring up on every city block. In post–Civil War Chicago, for example, there were more saloons than there were grocery and dry good stores combined. In 1887, Senator William Windom delivered an address describing the conditions he had observed in American cities:

> Every plausible temptation and solicitation that trained talent can suggest are used to entrap the young, the ignorant, the toiling, the homeless, with the knowledge that a customer once secured is usually a customer for life. . . . Experience indicates that four-fifths of American drinking and drunkenness is due in the first instance not to any natural appetite of our people, but to the presence and sleepless efforts of this gigantic enginery, working seven days a week and twenty-four hours a day, unrestrained by any scruple and everywhere contemptuous of public and private right.[1]

This proliferation of saloons did not escape the attention of two new temperance organizations that emerged in the latter half of the 1800s. The Woman's Christian Temperance Union (WCTU) and Anti-Saloon League (ASL) moved to the forefront of the fight with the support of influential business leaders who recognized the need for workers on their factory lines to be clearheaded and sober. Automobile industrialist Henry Ford was one of the staunchest supporters of sobriety and recognized that alcohol was not only a threat to the home, it threatened the national economy. He penned this stern warning to the *Pictorial Review:*

With booze in control we can count on only two or three effective days work a week in the factory—and that would destroy the short day and the five-day week which sober industry has introduced. When men were drunk two or three days a week, industry had to have a ten- or twelve-hour day and seven-day week. With sobriety the working man can have an eight-hour day and a five-day week with the same or greater pay. . . . I would not be able to build a car that will run 200,000 miles if booze were around, because I wouldn't have accurate workmen. To make these machines requires that the men increase their skill.[2]

Prohibition Becomes a National Issue

Between 1880 and the beginning of the First World War, a wave of temperance swept the nation. Writes author K. Austin Kerr, "One-half of the American population lived under some form of prohibition law. The state and local prohibition strategy was successful and now would be abetted by the new interstate shipment law. There was a solid core of dry support in Congress as more and more constituencies expressed their approval of prohibition."[3] After Congress passed the Webb-Kenyon Act in 1913 (which forbade the shipping of liquor into dry states), the Anti-Saloon League set their sights on national prohibition. They lobbied members of Congress to accept a "dry," or anti-alcohol, platform and worked their printing presses nonstop, grinding out dry literature to distribute in every congressional district.

The liquor interests responded with their own propaganda, mainly focusing on the economic loss Prohibition would incur. But their efforts could not match the huge campaign launched by the Anti-Saloon League. "Wet," or pro-alcohol, forces did not have the organization or leadership to rally and coordinate the support they could have gotten from the many Americans who opposed Prohibition. They also did not know how to respond to the patriotic and probusiness arguments being used against them by the Anti-Saloon League.

After the United States declared war on Germany in 1917, dry forces used wartime conservation as an excuse to ban grain supplies to the liquor industry. Drys argued that

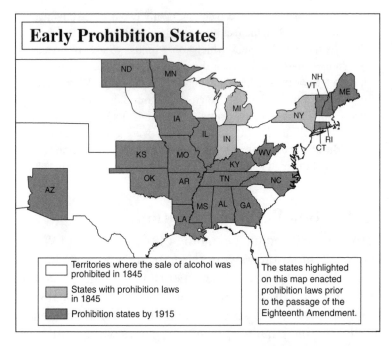

Early Prohibition States

ND
MN
NH
VT
ME
IA
MI
NY
IL
IN
RI
CT
KS
MO
WV
OK
AR
KY
TN
NC
AZ
MS
AL
GA
LA

☐ Territories where the sale of alcohol was prohibited in 1845

◩ States with prohibition laws in 1845

◼ Prohibition states by 1915

The states highlighted on this map enacted prohibition laws prior to the passage of the Eighteenth Amendment.

grain was wasted in the production of alcohol and should instead be conserved for food to feed America and its allies. The Anti-Saloon League also took advantage of growing anti-German sentiment. They promoted beer as being un-American and repeatedly reminded the public that the majority of brewing interests were owned by Germans (who had flooded into America during the last wave of immigration). They even challenged brewery owner loyalty with unfounded accusations, prompting Senate investigations and big headlines. Some German American organizations were even asked to disband, which gave the Anti-Saloon League's accusations an air of validity.

The Eighteenth Amendment

With dry sentiment running high, the Eighteenth Amendment was adopted by Congress on August 1917. President Woodrow Wilson supported the concept of temperance but had vetoed the amendment because he believed it was ethically unsound and constitutionally invalid. But Congress overrode the president's veto on the same day. The Eighteenth Amendment was quickly passed by an overwhelming margin in both the Senate and House of Representatives. Since many states already had dry laws in place, ratification only took a year. This still surprised both wets and drys who thought it would take three or four years. With the amendment passed, Prohibition was set to become the law of the land in 1920.

The National Prohibition Act, more commonly known as the Volstead Act, followed on October 28, 1919. The bill, which incorporated the best features of successful state prohibition laws, specified how the federal law would be enforced. It was named after its sponsor, Andrew Volstead, a conservative Minnesota congressman. But it was Anti-Saloon League lobbyist Wayne B. Wheeler who actually drafted the original legislation and all of its weaknesses. Volstead and others had recognized early on that there were problems with the bill. Prohibition leader Bishop Canon William Sheafe Chase had pointed out, "The Volstead Act is full of loopholes. The wets know the loopholes. The drys generally do not know them. They have accepted the wet propaganda that the Volstead Act is very drastic and despotic and that the experience of the dry states in enforcing Prohibition was incorporated into the National Prohibition Act."[4] But the hope was that the rough points would be ironed out down the line.

One of the most controversial points was the bill's definition of an intoxicating beverage. The law stated that anything with more than one-half of 1 percent alcohol by volume was illegal. This surprised many moderate supporters of Prohibition who thought beer and wine would be exempted. But the limit was set to prevent the legal distribution of all alcohol. At least brewers had a choice. They could stay in business if they chose to brew "near beer." Near beer was beer that had most of the alcohol boiled off during the brewing process. The brewers knew the taste was not the same as real beer and those that did sell near beer delivered the product to customers with a separate—and illegal—package that contained a portion of raw alcohol that could be reintroduced into the drink.

Another contentious issue concerned the Prohibition

agents that had been hired to enforce the law. Few, if any, had qualifications. They were exempt from any minimum standards required for a civil service position. Historian Edward Behr writes becoming a Prohibition agent had nothing to do with what you knew but who you knew: "All that was required on the part of an aspiring Prohibition agent was the endorsement of the ASL, a congressman, or other prominent local politician. No other qualifications or character references were needed; some of the new recruits even had criminal records."[5] Additionally, low pay contributed to high turnover and widespread corruption that would plague the Prohibition Bureau until repeal.

The Final Toast

On January 15, 1920, a day before the law took effect, a federal judge declared that all liquor found outside the privacy of home could be confiscated. This caused a panic on the streets as millions of people across the country, who for weeks had been stockpiling private supplies of liquor in warehouses and safe deposit boxes, were now forced to take their reserves home. Speaking of New York, author Thomas M. Coffey writes that anything with wheels was commandeered, "Here, as in most other cities, the streets had been filled with cars, trucks, taxis, wagons, and even baby buggies, all carrying heavy loads of bottled goods. Pedestrians had burdened themselves with as much as they could lift."[6]

Saloon keepers who were faced with being on the wrong side of the law slashed their prices. A few even gave away liquor since those who were not able to clear their shelves had it done for them by eager Prohibition agents wielding bats and sledgehammers. Overall, the expected widespread drunkenness of last minute revelers did not happen. Instead, most of the drinking public stayed home to mourn the loss. It was the overjoyed prohibitionists who would celebrate the loudest over the first few days of the ban. Towns all over the nation rang their church bells. Evangelist Billy Sunday presided over a mock funeral for John Barleycorn (a mythical figure who symbolized the evils of alcohol) that included a twenty-foot coffin and a train of horses. Once a heavy drinker himself, Sunday gave an unsympathetic eulogy before ten thousand prohibitionists: "Good-bye, John. You were God's worst enemy. You were Hell's best friend. I hate you with the perfect hatred."[7]

Getting Around the Law

The nation may have been declared dry but Americans had no trouble finding other ways to slake their thirst. Lawmakers underestimated the spirit of innovation that Prohibition would inspire. For example, the Volstead Act contained exemptions that allowed for alcohol to be used for industrial purposes as well as for religious and medical use. Lawyer George Remus became rich exploiting this exception. Invoking a bit of creative foresight, Remus used his savings to purchase whiskey certificates, distilleries, and pharmacies so he could sell alcohol, under government license, for "medicinal" purposes. Remus was estimated to have made $40 million before he was caught.

Prohibition also created opportunities for fishermen and boat owners. The lengths of the Canadian and Mexican borders could not be adequately patrolled, and that tempted many fishermen who were experiencing hard times to transport illegal liquor into the United States. There was also Rum Row, which sat outside the three-mile limit of U.S. waters (which was later extended to twelve miles). Rum Row was where ships from other countries brought liquor to sell. The purchase was legal outside the U.S. limit, and fishermen and other boat owners made money bringing landlubbers out to the foreign ships. Aggressive Prohibition and Coast Guard units often fired on vessels that strayed into U.S. waters.

For those who did not take to the high seas, drugstores sold the Grape Brick, which was a block of dried wine grape concentrate. This do-it-yourself concoction was usually sold with a packet of yeast and a label that warned users not to combine the two with water or else wine would be the result. Of course, few heeded the warning. Hardware stores also contributed to the delinquency of the law by advertising all the equipment needed to set up a still at home. Most of these kits could make about a gallon of alcohol at a time from fruits, grains, potato peelings, and anything else containing sugar that could be fermented. For larger batches, the bathtub could be converted into a makeshift still, giving rise to the term bathtub gin. The Prohibition Bureau estimated that as much as 700 million gallons of liquor was produced by such means in 1929.

A large part of the alcohol circulating around dry America was denatured. Denatured alcohol was alcohol made poisonous by the government who added methanol or other chemicals. It was meant to discourage consumption, but with a little patience a determined bootlegger could convert denatured alcohol into something drinkable if not necessarily good tasting. In the boweries of big cities like New York, desperate people who could not afford to buy decent quality bootleg liquor drank whatever they could find, including isopropyl (rubbing) alcohol. It was not uncommon to find dead bodies slumped over a bottle in alleyways. Contribut-

Prohibition agents pour bootleg whiskey down a sewer. It was estimated that 95 percent of bootleg alcohol contained poisons.

ing to the problem was the lack of mandatory poison labels. The Anti-Saloon League had lobbied against warning labels and was criticized by the press for it. The ASL disclaimed responsibility for any deaths in a press release. "The government is under no obligation to supply alcohol that is drinkable when the Constitution prohibits it," they argued, and then added, "The person who drinks this industrial alcohol is a deliberate suicide."[8]

While bootlegging was certainly profitable, other businesses also sprang up as a result of Prohibition. The saloon may have been forever banished but its spirit was reborn in the speakeasy. Speakeasies were underground bars that operated in secret locations. Because of its clandestine atmosphere, the speakeasy gave birth to a new underground culture. Here social customs fell by the wayside. For example, many women who previously would have felt excluded in a saloon freely drank and smoked in the speakeasy. According to author Martin Hintz, "the speakeasy opened the door to a different world, one that shattered old-time barriers in morals and manners."[9] All of these establishments catered to a diverse clientele including artists, celebrities, and politicians of the wet and dry persuasion. Some speakeasies, like the Stork Club, were also good restaurants and nightclubs that would survive many closures and become legitimate establishments after repeal.

Crime in America

Although the dark legacy of organized crime has been attributed to Prohibition, gangs were well established far before the passage of the Eighteenth Amendment. The enormous profit that could be gained from bootlegging just prompted crime lords to partake of the wealth. In the major cities, competition between rival gangs provoked bloody turf wars that made headlines and gave the impression that Prohibition had caused the growth of crime. In Chicago, one of the most violently contested cities in the country, authorities reported 350 to 400 gangland murders per year. Many of these murders took place in public. It gave Chicago the reputation for being the most gang-ridden city in the country.

Italian-born Al "Scarface" Capone was the best-known gangster of the era. He was thought of more as a celebrity than a criminal partly due to the unpopularity of the Prohibition laws. Capone also understood the value of good press and tended to be generous with his money in public. He tipped well, gave money to children, and even opened up a soup kitchen in Chicago. Of course, all of his philanthropy was a smoke screen to conceal his bootlegging activities.

Capone's popularity turned on Valentine's Day of 1929. The event was the climax of a protracted war between the O'Banion and Capone gangs. Several men dressed as police officers entered the garage where seven members of the O'Banion gang were setting up to do morning business. The unsuspecting gangsters were all put up against the wall in what looked like a routine police raid. But the seven O'Banion men were executed by submachine-gun fire. Nobody was charged or convicted. The leader of the O'Banion gang, Bugs Moran, had overslept that morning and was not at the garage. He knew Capone was responsible and vowed revenge. Capone wisely chose to lay low and arranged to have himself arrested on a gun-possession charge in Florida. He was sent to prison for a short time. Capone was responsible for many murders and other serious crimes but he was never indicted for any of them. His most serious charge would be tax evasion for which he again went to prison. He died in 1947 a free man.

By the mid-1920s, many Americans in Chicago and other cities were fed up with the corruption and violence wrought by Prohibition. The homicide rate was up 75 percent, but it was the minor violations of the Volstead Act that would clog the legal system and fill overcrowded prisons. Much of the problem could be attributed to lack of cooperation amongst competing enforcement agencies, widespread corruption, and the connivance of high-level Washington politicians. Even the president of the United States, Warren Harding, was involved in scandal. In 1920, Harding had brought a group of his friends to Washington when he became president. These men, who had been nicknamed the Ohio Gang, took advantage of Harding's trusting nature by issuing liquor permits and granting other illegal favors behind his back. One of his appointees, Charles Forbes, was discovered to have swindled the nation out of hundreds of millions of dollars during World War I. His secretary of the interior and close friend, Albert Fall, was caught trying to mastermind an oil scheme that became known as the Teapot Dome Scandal. Harding died in 1923 as the scandal broke but the investigations would continue for years afterward, contributing to the country's deepening disillusionment of Prohibition.

The Wet Revival

It was not long before even die-hard drys could see that Prohibition was failing. The amount of crime and political corruption seemed to increase every year. The number of speakeasies and liquor outlets was multiplying despite the increased efforts of Prohibition authorities. With no licensing hassles, everybody could become a bootlegger. A New York newspaper assigned a team of reporters to find out how easy it was to find liquor in Manhattan. They published the following list of sources for illegal drink: "Dancing academies, drugstores, delicatessens, cigar stores, confectioners, soda fountains, behind partitions of shoeshine parlors, back rooms of barbershops, from hotel bellhops, from hotel headwaiters, night clerks, in express offices, in motorcycle delivery agencies, paint stores, malt shops, cider stubes, fruit stands, vegetable markets, groceries, smoke shops, athletic clubs, grill rooms, taverns, chophouses, importing firms, tearooms, moving-van companies, spaghetti houses, boarding houses, Republican clubs, Democratic clubs, laundries, social clubs, newspapermen's associations."[10] All of this amounted to hundreds of millions in lost liquor tax revenue with little benefit to society.

Influential people were coming out to speak in favor of repeal, including many formerly dry politicians. But the seeming impossibility in repealing a constitutional amendment was daunting to the wets. A constitutional amendment had never been repealed in the history of the country because it required a two-thirds majority in the House and Senate. The famous defense attorney Clarence Darrow, who opposed Prohibition, was quoted as saying a summer vacation on Mars was more likely.

One of the most influential wet organizations to rally behind repeal was the Association Against the Prohibition Amendment (AAPA). The AAPA was formed in 1922 after the Volstead Act was ratified and became a counterpart to the Anti-Saloon League. The organization's ranks were composed of business leaders who feared that personal and corporate taxes would be hiked up to make up for the loss of liquor tax revenue. The AAPA adopted the same tactics used by the Anti-Saloon League in supporting any candidate, regardless of party, who sided with their repeal efforts. The AAPA also launched a massive propaganda campaign that rivaled any put out by any dry organization. The AAPA was well funded and had no problems matching the Anti-Saloon League.

Another wet movement that worked hard to bring about repeal was the Woman's Organization for National Prohibition Reform (WONPR). The WONPR was similar to the Woman's Christian Temperance Union in that both organizations were started by determined women working on behalf of other women. The WONPR was founded in 1929 by Pauline Sabine and a group of other like-minded women who composed the who's who of high society in the 1920s.

Many women joined WONPR just so they could hobnob with society's elite. Membership quickly grew from one hundred thousand to three hundred thousand with active chapters in thirty-three states. One of the most effective WONPR campaign methods was for members to go door-to-door to win support. They especially focused on rural areas that were entrenched with Prohibition's core supporters. Although they had many doors slammed in their faces, they were also able to win many converts. Another effective method the WONPR employed was to deluge politicians with letters and telegrams urging them to support repeal.

Their campaign netted over 250 favorable replies, including one from presidential candidate Franklin Roosevelt.

The Downward Slide

In 1929 the stock market crashed and sent the nation spinning into a major depression. Over the next few years, businesses and banks across the nation closed and sent unemployment to unprecedented heights. The wet propagandists used the economic troubles as a focal point of their repeal. Wets blamed Prohibition for making the depression worse. They claimed it took away badly needed jobs and deprived the government of revenue that could have been gotten from taxes on liquor. They also blamed Prohibition for exacerbating the farm crisis. Shutting down the liquor industry deprived farmers, who sold grain supplies such as hops and barley, of their market. As the depression worsened and breadlines got longer, President Herbert Hoover's inadequate relief measures just added to the nation's growing frustration with Prohibition. Combined with wet propaganda, it made repeal an important—although secondary— issue in the 1932 elections.

Repeal

After Franklin Roosevelt accepted his party's nomination for president in 1932, he spoke before the Democratic Convention and said, "This convention wants repeal. Your candidate wants repeal. And I am confident that the United States wants repeal. From this date on, the Eighteenth Amendment is doomed!"[11] The response was thundering and the promise brought new converts to the wet cause. Former dry activist John D. Rockefeller Jr. resignedly sent a letter to the *New York Times* which publicly announced his support of repeal. Industrialist Pierre du Pont and newspaper magnate William Randolph Hearst also added their considerable influence. In fact, Hearst employed his chain of newspapers to preach the pros of repeal.

Nine days after taking office, Roosevelt cut funding for the Prohibition Bureau and asked Congress to modify the

Volstead Act's definition of an "intoxicating beverage." Congress speedily complied and agreed on 3.2 percent alcohol by volume. Beer drinkers celebrated this victory with parades and processions. Fifty thousand people were said to have filled the streets in front of breweries in St. Louis and Milwaukee. In other parts of the country people jammed restaurants, hotels, and nightclubs for their first legal drink of real beer in thirteen years. One and a half million barrels of beer were consumed in the first twenty-four hours. The APAA helped Roosevelt put through a resolution to repeal the Eighteenth Amendment which still stood. It was met with very little resistance and quickly passed by the necessary two-thirds ratification within a year, just as the previous amendment had. Prohibition ended on December 5, 1933. A few states, mostly in the South, retained Prohibition until the 1950s and 1960s, but even Mississippi, which held out until 1966, eventually gave in to the people's wishes.

The crowds that had been predicted would fill the streets in drunken celebration of repeal never appeared. In most cities it was police officers, mobilized in anticipation, who patrolled empty streets. This was because most speakeasies, which flooded the Prohibition Bureau with applications for licenses, had yet to become legitimate establishments, through due process. And the brewers and distillers, who had stood idle for over a decade, would have a lot of catching up to do to meet the enormous demand.

The effects of Prohibition, however, would still not be stricken from the record with repeal. The problem of alcohol abuse remained unsolved. But the dry laws did provide a valuable lesson. Prohibition showed that trying to control human behavior with legislation did not work. Edward Behr writes, "The moralists and evangelical pioneers without whom Prohibition would have remained a dead letter believed that enactment of the Eighteenth Amendment would be sufficient to change the habits of American society as a whole. They were quickly proved disastrously wrong."[12] Prohibition also brought a new understanding of the addictive quality of alcohol. Alcoholics Anonymous (AA) was founded in 1935 as a direct result. AA is an organization that empowered alcoholics with the understanding of their addiction and what is needed to control it. Alcoholics Anonymous is still around today giving support and helping millions of people control their vice.

Notes

1. Quoted in Fletcher Dobyns, *The Amazing Story of Repeal*. Chicago: Willett, Clark, 1940, p. 233.

2. Quoted in Edward Behr, *Prohibition: Thirteen Years That Changed America*. New York: Arcade, 1996, p. 150.

3. K. Austin Kerr, *Organized for Prohibition: A New History of the Anti-Saloon League*. New Haven, CT: Yale University Press, 1985, p. 138.

4. Quoted in Dobyns, *The Amazing Story of Repeal*, p. 2.

5. Behr, *Prohibition: Thirteen Years That Changed America*, p. 83.

6. Thomas M. Coffey, *The Long Thirst: Prohibition in America: 1920–1933*. New York: W.W. Norton, 1975, p. 3.

7. Quoted in *New York Times*, January 17, 1920, p. 3.

8. Quoted in Behr, *Prohibition: Thirteen Years That Changed America*, p. 222.

9. Martin Hintz, *Farewell, John Barleycorn: Prohibition in the United States*. Minneapolis: Lerner, 1996, p. 55.

10. Quoted in John Kobler, *Ardent Spirits*. New York: G.P. Putnam's Sons, 1973, p. 255.

11. Quoted in Bill Severn, *The End of the Roaring Twenties: Prohibition and Repeal*. New York: Julian Messner, 1969, p. 172.

12. Behr, *Prohibition: Thirteen Years That Changed America*, p. 8.

Chapter 1

The Drys

Chapter Preface

The Eighteenth Amendment was the end result of a forty-year crusade. In that period many colorful individuals and temperance organizations rose to meet the challenge of persuading the nation to accept Prohibition. Many of these organizations were run by determined women such as Frances Elizabeth Willard, the president of the Woman's Christian Temperance Union. The WCTU became one of the first large-scale women's movements in the United States, promoting other social issues as well as Prohibition. Such advocates met little resistance, as anti-Prohibition, or wet, forces were mostly disorganized in the early days of the debate.

The most powerful temperance organization of all time was the Anti-Saloon League. The ASL utilized a two-prong attack: lobbying politicians while simultaneously educating the masses on the evils of alcohol. They produced millions of pieces of literature, which saturated American schools and political offices. The purpose was to effect national prohibition at all costs. Unfortunately, the single-mindedness of the ASL also led to its downfall. The ASL had been created to establish national prohibition and had not formulated an agenda for a dry America. After the passage of the Eighteenth Amendment, many within the ASL believed the battle had not been finished, but they had no plan for further social change. Support started to drop away, along with vital funding. Eventually the internal conflicts between competing members almost led to the league's dissolution. This loss of power and the ASL's lack of clear goals contributed to Prohibition's ignoble defeat in the coming years.

The Evils of Alcohol

Billy Sunday

> Billy Sunday was a popular evangelist of the teens and twenties
> and one of the most outspoken figures of the "dry" movement.
> He strongly believed temperance would rid society of crime
> and poverty. Sunday traveled around the country preaching
> against the evils of alcoholism. He spoke before packed houses
> and was known to draw crowds of fifty thousand people. The
> following selection is taken from his popular "booze" sermon
> in which his arguments and statistics were not unimpeachable,
> but his colorful language and showmanship made them seem
> convincing enough to his God-fearing audiences. This particu-
> lar version of the speech was delivered in 1913, but it was
> repeated throughout the era of Prohibition debate.
>
> Sunday returned to preaching after realizing repeal was
> inevitable. But his popularity had waned due to his associa-
> tion with Prohibition and its failure. Sunday never recovered
> the audiences he had during the twenties. He died in Illinois
> in 1935.

The saloon is the sum of all villainies. It is worse than
war or pestilence. It is the crime of crimes. It is the parent of crimes and the mother of sins. It is the appalling
source of misery and crime in the land. And to license such
an incarnate fiend of hell is the dirtiest, low-down, damnable
business on top of this old earth. There is nothing to be compared to it.

The legislature of Illinois appropriated $6,000,000 in
1908 to take care of the insane people in the state, and the

Excerpted from *"Billy" Sunday: The Man and His Message*, by William T. Ellis (Swath-
more, PA: L.T. Myers, 1914).

whisky business produces seventy-five per cent of the insane. That is what you go down in your pockets for to help support. Do away with the saloons and you will close these institutions. The saloons make them necessary, and they make the poverty and fill the jails and the penitentiaries. Who has to pay the bills? The landlord who doesn't get the rent because the money goes for whisky; the butcher and the grocer and the charitable person who takes pity on the children of drunkards, and the taxpayer who supports the insane asylums and other institutions, that the whisky business keeps full of human wrecks.

Do away with the cursed business and you will not have to put up to support them. Who gets the money? The saloon-keepers and the brewers, and the distillers, while the whisky fills the land with misery, and poverty, and wretchedness, and disease, and death, and damnation, and it is being authorized by the will of the sovereign people.

Booze Arguments

You say that "people will drink anyway." Not by my vote. You say, "Men will murder their wives anyway." Not by my vote. "They will steal anyway." Not by my vote. You are the sovereign people, and what are you going to do about it?

Let me assemble before your minds the bodies of the drunken dead, who crawl away "into the jaws of death, into the mouth of hell," and then out of the valley of the shadow of the drink let me call the appertaining motherhood, and wifehood, and childhood, and let their tears rain down upon their purple faces. Do you think that would stop the curse of the liquor traffic? No! No!

In these days when the question of saloon or no saloon is at the fore in almost every community, one hears a good deal about what is called "personal liberty." These are fine, large, mouth-filling words, and they certainly do sound first rate; but when you get right down and analyze them in the light of common old horse-sense, you will discover that in their application to the present controversy they mean just about this: "Personal liberty" is for the man who, if he has the inclination and the price, can stand up at a bar and fill his hide so full of red liquor that he is transformed for the time being into an irresponsible, dangerous, evil-smelling brute. But "personal liberty" is not for his patient, long-suffering wife, who has to endure with what fortitude she may his blows and curses; nor is it for his children, who, if they escape his insane rage, are yet robbed of every known joy and privilege of childhood, and too often grow up neglected, uncared for and vicious as the result of their surroundings and the example before them. "Personal liberty" is not for the sober, industrious citizen who from the proceeds of honest toil and orderly living, has to pay, willingly or not, the tax bills which pile up as a direct result of drunkenness, disorder and poverty, the items of which are written in the records of every police court and poorhouse in the land; nor is "personal liberty" for the good woman who goes

The Wrath of Carry Nation

The wife of an unsuccessful preacher, Carry Nation was a fierce foe of the liquor industry, writes Edward Behr, author of the book Prohibition: Thirteen Years That Changed America. *Nation believed God had spoken with her and sent her to destroy illegal saloons that operated in open defiance of the law. Symbolized by the ax she carried, Carry Nation became feared by saloon owners all over the country during Prohibition.*

Back in Medicine Lodge [Kansas], she bought a large hatchet—an instrument of destruction that was to become her emblem, and enrich the American vocabulary with the word *hatchetization*. Her message was now painfully direct: "Smash! Smash! For Jesus' sake, smash!"

In a series of raids all over Kansas, she continued the good work, leaving in her wake wrecked cherrywood bars, smashed plate glass windows, and slashed, defaced paintings—"hatchetizing" kegs of rum and whiskey and reducing heavy barroom furniture to firewood. Her raids were so sudden, her violence so frightening, that few dared face her directly.

abroad in the town only at the risk of being shot down by some drink-crazed creature. This rant about "personal liberty" as an argument has no leg to stand upon. . . .

The Economic Side

Now listen! Last year the income of the United States government, and the cities and towns and counties, from the whisky business was $350,000,000. That is putting it liberally. You say that's a lot of money. Well, last year the working men spent $2,000,000,000 for drink, and it cost $1,200,000,000 to care for the judicial machinery. In other words, the whisky business cost us last year $3,400,000,000. I will subtract from that the dirty $350,000,000 which we got, and it leaves $3,050,000,000 in favor of knocking the whisky business out on purely a money basis. And listen! We spend $6,000,000,000 a year for our paupers and crim-

---

Local authorities were in a quandary: though she was inflicting huge losses on saloon keepers, the saloons (or "joints") were, after all, unauthorized. She was, admittedly illegally, destroying valuable property, but the property was part and parcel of an illicit activity. Consequently, she seldom spent more than one night in jail, and reveled in the publicity—posing, kneeling in her cell, conversing with Jesus, and clasping a Bible as press photographers crowded around her. The jailers became her friends, for she was also capable of considerable charm.

Kansas was soon too small for her. Soon she was showing up, always without warning, all over America, wrecking saloons in St. Louis, Cincinnati (where she refrained from hatchetization; the joints, she claimed, simply too numerous), Philadelphia, and New York. She became, overnight, a media star. Songs were written about her, and saloon keepers, dreading her hit-and-run tactics, securely padlocked their establishments until she was known to have left town.

Edward Behr, *Prohibition: Thirteen Years That Changed America.* New York: Arcade Publishing, 1996.

inals, insane, orphans, feeble-minded, etc., and eighty-two per cent of our criminals are whisky-made, and seventy-five per cent of the paupers are whisky-made. The average factory hand earns $450 a year, and it costs us $1,200 a year to support each of our whisky criminals. There are 326,000 enrolled criminals in the United States and 80,000 in jails and penitentiaries. Three-fourths were sent there because of drink, and then they have the audacity to say the saloon is needed for money revenue. Never was there a baser lie.

"But," says the whisky fellow, "we would lose trade; the farmer would not come to town to trade." You lie. I am a farmer. I was born and raised on a farm and I have the malodors of the barnyard on me today. Yes, sir. And when you say that you insult the best class of men on God's dirt. Say, when you put up the howl that if you don't have the saloons the farmer won't trade—say, Mr. Whisky Man, why do you dump money into politics and back the legislatures into the corner and fight to the last ditch to prevent the enactment of county local option? You know if the farmers were given a chance they would knock the whisky business into hell the first throw out of the box. You are afraid. You have cold feet on the proposition. You are afraid to give the farmer a chance. They are scared to death of you farmers. . . .

And say, my friends, New York City's annual drink bill is $365,000,000 a year, $1,000,000 a day. Listen a minute. That is four times the annual output of gold, and six times the value of all the silver mined in the United States. And in New York there is one saloon for every thirty families. The money spent in New York by the working people for drink in ten years would buy every working man in New York a beautiful home, allowing $3,500 for house and lot. It would take fifty persons one year to count the money in $1 bills, and they would cover 10,000 acres of ground. That is what the people in New York dump into the whisky hole in one year. And then you wonder why there is poverty and crime, and that the country is not more prosperous. . . .

The American mongoose is the open licensed saloon. It eats the carpets off the floor and the clothes from off your back, your money out of the bank, and it eats up character, and it goes on until at last it leaves a stranded wreck in the home, a skeleton of what was once brightness and happiness.

There were some men playing cards on a railroad train, and one fellow pulled out a whisky flask and passed it about, and when it came to the drummer he said, "No." "What," they said, "have you got on the water wagon?" and they all laughed at him. He said, "You can laugh if you want to, but I was born with an appetite for drink, and for years I have taken from five to ten glasses per day, but I was at home in Chicago not long ago and I have a friend who has a pawn shop there. I was in there when in came a young fellow with ashen cheeks and a wild look on his face. He came up trembling, threw down a little package and said, 'Give me ten cents.' And what do you think was in that package? It was a pair of baby shoes.

"My friend said, 'No, I cannot take them.'

"'But,' he said, 'give me a dime. I must have a drink.'

"'No, take them back home, your baby will need them.'

"And the poor fellow said, 'My baby is dead, and I want a drink.'"

Boys, I don't blame you for the lump that comes up in your throat. There is no law, divine or human, that the saloon respects. Lincoln said, "If slavery is not wrong, nothing is wrong." I say, if the saloon, with its train of diseases, crime and misery, is not wrong, then nothing on earth is wrong. If the fight is to be won we need men—men that will fight—the Church, Catholic and Protestant, must fight it or run away, and thank God she will not run away, but fight to the last ditch. . . .

"The Saloon Is a Coward"

As Dr. [Clinton] Howard said: "I tell you that the saloon is a coward." It hides itself behind stained-glass doors and opaque windows, and sneaks its customers in at a blind door, and it keeps a sentinel to guard the door from the officers of the law, and it marks its wares with false bills-of-lading, and offers to ship green goods to you and marks them with the name of wholesome articles of food so people won't know what is being sent to you. And so vile did that business get that the legislature of Indiana passed a law forbidding a saloon to ship goods without being properly labeled. And the United States Congress passed a law forbidding them to send whisky through the mails.

I tell you it strikes in the night. It fights under cover of darkness and assassinates the characters that it cannot damn, and it lies about you. It attacks defenseless womanhood and childhood. The saloon is a coward. It is a thief; it is not an ordinary court offender that steals your money, but it robs you of manhood and leaves you in rags and takes away your friends, and it robs your family. It impoverishes your children and it brings insanity and suicide. It will take the shirt off your back and it will steal the coffin from a dead child and yank the last crust of bread out of the hand of the starving child; it will take the last bucket of coal out of your cellar, and the last cent out of your pocket, and will send you home bleary-eyed and staggering to your wife and children. It will steal the milk from the breast of the mother and leave her with nothing with which to feed her infant. It will take the virtue from your daughter. It is the dirtiest, most lowdown, damnable business that ever crawled out of the pit of hell. It is a sneak, and a thief and a coward.

It is an infidel. It has no faith in God; has no religion. It would close every church in the land. It would hang its beer signs on the abandoned altars. It would close every public school. It respects the thief and it esteems the blasphemer; it fills the prisons and the penitentiaries. It despises heaven, hates love, scorns virtue. It tempts the passions. Its music is the song of a siren. Its sermons are a collection of lewd, vile stories. It wraps a mantle about the hope of this world and that to come. Its tables are full of the vilest literature. It is the moral clearing house for rot, and damnation, and poverty, and insanity, and it wrecks homes and blights lives today.

Give Prohibition Its Chance

Ella A. Boole

From the beginning, temperance was viewed as a woman's cause. Women had traditionally been cast as protectors of the home, and alcohol abuse threatened family life. But dealing with the problem solely within the household proved to be ineffective. The Woman's Christian Temperance Union (WCTU) was founded in 1874 by a group of women who wanted to make the alcohol problem a public concern. Members took the battle onto the streets in marches, protests, and rallies. They even lobbied lawmakers in Washington, D.C. The WCTU eventually achieved its ultimate goal of bringing about national prohibition. But by the late twenties, the threat of repeal loomed over every dry's head.

Ella A. Boole was president of the WCTU from 1925 to 1933. The following selection is from her book, *Give Prohibition Its Chance*. By the time it was published, it was obvious to everybody that the widespread disregard for the law was responsible for its failing. A law could not be enforced if everybody was an accomplice to the crime. In her book, she makes a plea for public cooperation in making Prohibition work.

We believe prohibition is the best method of dealing with the liquor traffic. We appeal to the American public to give it a chance by obeying the law voluntarily. We appeal to the press for loyalty to the Constitution and editorial support of this method adopted after long years of education

Excerpted from *Give Prohibition Its Chance*, by Ella A. Boole (Evanston, IL: National Woman's Christian Temperance Union, 1929).

and by the orderly processes of government. We appeal to that patriotism which rallies to the support of the government when it is attacked by a foreign foe, to rally to the support of the government when attacked by a foe from within.

We did not believe that enforcement would be bettered if placed in the hands of its enemies, in the hands of those who wanted to destroy or nullify it. Therefore we entered into politics with the single purpose of electing a Dry President and Vice-President, and Dry members of Congress, that enforcement might be placed in the hands of those who wanted to make it a success and legislation entrusted to a Congress which would conserve the Eighteenth Amendment and the Volstead Act.

With increased emphasis, we continue our educational work to the end that the people may willingly obey the law, and the officials may be supported in the performance of their duties.

Give prohibition its chance. Law enforcement is a question of politics and citizenship. The honest efforts of officials charged with the responsibility for law enforcement should be supported by the pulpit, the press and the people, but the United States will not receive full benefit of the law unless the pulpit, the press and the people support law observance as well. By this we mean the spirit as well as the letter of the Eighteenth Amendment.

The object of prohibition was to protect the American home from the drink traffic and the drink habit.

Educating and Setting Examples

The drink traffic is an outlaw.

The drink habit remains and this is created and fostered by the use of alcoholic liquors whether they are sold legally or illegally. The drink habit must be destroyed. It can only be destroyed by total abstinence. I hereby call upon all women to discourage through a campaign of education the use of intoxicating liquor. Not every one knows that alcohol is a narcotic poison which taken in small quantities has the power to create the appetite for more. We must explain that there is a reason for the prohibition of the beverage traffic in intoxicating liquors and with renewed emphasis we must bring the teaching of science to our aid to promote willing obedience to the law. We must continue to show the effect of alcohol on child welfare. We must make it clear that money spent for drink too often robs the home of necessities. We must show the degeneracy caused by drink. We must show the loss in mental power. We must show the loss in health. We must show the waste in money.

With emphasis we must place the responsibility where it belongs upon society leaders who maintain the social standards of wine-drinking countries even though they know that such standards cannot be maintained without purchas-

This Currier and Ives illustration depicts the nineteenth-century crusade for temperance and Prohibition.

ing liquor of a bootlegger and so helping to finance him.

Special privileges allowed foreign diplomats in Washington of importing liquors for use of themselves and their employees and so giving them the legal right to maintain in America foreign social standards are productive of great harm and should be abolished. We rather like the attitude of a great General in the World War who, when he was in this country, refused to drink intoxicating liquors out of respect to the law of the nation.

We appeal to native-born Americans to set foreigners, whether their stay here be long or short, such an example that they will know they are not welcome to our country unless they accept our laws and obey them. They should not take advantage of our better wages and better standards of living unless they are willing to accept our laws. Let us urge all organizations and religious bodies which have passed resolutions for law enforcement to recognize obedience to the Eighteenth Amendment as an integral part of law enforcement.

Let us give prohibition a chance by expecting all who talk dry and vote dry to live dry, by obeying the law at their clubs, in their hotels, at their places of business and in their homes.

A Moral Obligation

Law observance is a moral obligation. It is personal and individual. In the early days of New England when municipal lighting of streets was unheard of, each householder hung a lantern outside his door to light the steps of his fellow-men. At the call of fire the men and boys rushed to the scene of disaster and the women threw buckets from their doors and windows into the street that the men might not be delayed. They too helped. The community was protected and safeguarded from home to home.

Let us now appeal to the citizens of our country to make a great bulwark of protection against the liquor traffic from *home* to *home*. To this end, willing obedience to the law is necessary.

Give prohibition a chance personally and politically. The liquor traffic had its day.

Prohibition for the Common Good

Charles Stelzle

> Charles Stelzle was a journalist, an advocate for the Pres-
> byterian Church, and a prohibitionist. In his book *Why
> Prohibition!* Stelzle writes that alcohol must be banished
> or civilization cannot grow. In the following excerpt from a
> chapter of his book, he provides a counterargument to anti-
> prohibitionists who argue Prohibition infringes on the rights
> of the individual. Stelzle held that every individual in a mod-
> ern society sacrifices liberties for the good of the people as a
> whole. The health of society outweighs the individual's right
> to indulge in alcoholic beverages. Many prominent leaders of
> industry, such as Henry Ford and John D. Rockefeller Jr.,
> supported Stelzle's view.

The doctrine of "personal liberty" as applied to the use
of liquor has been over-worked by the liquor men. As a
matter of fact, there is no such thing as an absolute individual right to do any particular thing, or to eat or drink any
particular thing, or to enjoy the association of one's own
family, or even to live, if that thing is in conflict with "the
law of public necessity."

If a member of your family becomes ill with a highly
contagious disease he is quarantined—no one is allowed to
visit him excepting those who minister to his needs.

When a great fire breaks out in a congested district, build-

Excerpted from *Why Prohibition!* by Charles Stelzle (New York: George H. Doran Company, 1918).

ings surrounding the fire are blown up in order to prevent the further spread of the fire.

These measures are resorted to for the common good.

For the Welfare of Society as a Whole

We are told by the liquor men that the State has no right to tell you whom you shall marry. . . .

Suppose you were to select as your wife an imbecile or a lunatic? Legislation on this point isn't quite so far along as it might be, but there's no doubt that soon there will be complete prohibition in this respect, in order to help wipe out imbecility and lunacy.

You can't marry your cousin in some states; you can't marry your sister in any state, and you will find it difficult to marry a divorced woman under some circumstances.

Furthermore, if the present tendency in the matter of eugenics[1] is continued, you'll have to be a fairly perfect human specimen if you wish to marry any woman.

You'll have to be free from disease and some other handicaps which might result in the increase of disease, before you can get a marriage license.

This will often prove to be a real hardship, and there's a danger of carrying the application of the laws of eugenics too far, but in all this prohibition there's just one consideration—*the welfare of society as a whole.*

It is insisted that the physical and moral weaknesses of mankind must not be perpetuated through the children born of defective parents. The State declares that it must protect itself against such misfortune, no matter how much some individuals may suffer.

It is quite apparent that as civilisation advances, society or the State will lay heavier obligations upon all individuals composing the State, even to the point of the sacrifice of one's most precious "personal liberty." For it is only thus that society itself can serve all individuals, giving each a larger measure of life and happiness. . . .

---

1. The science of improving the human race through selective breeding; it fell into disfavor after Hitler and the National Socialist Party subverted its principles.

Liquor Is Harmful to the Individual and Society

Liquor men tell us that one man has as much right to drink a glass of whiskey as another has to drink a cup of tea, but you never heard of one man killing another while he was under the influence of tea, and this fact does have something to do with the question of what a man has a right to drink.

You are not permitted to spend your wages as you please if you have a family to support—you must first provide for your family.

You are not permitted to keep your backyard or your kitchen or your cellar in a bad sanitary condition, because by so doing you would endanger the lives and health of your neighbors.

You are not permitted to keep your children out of school, even though you yourself do not believe in education, because these children also belong to the State and it is the wish of the State to make them good citizens, so it insists upon compulsory education.

You are not permitted to use habit-forming drugs, because, among other reasons, if you do so, you may make yourself a burden to the State.

A noted defender of the saloon recently said, "the State trusts you with the liberty to kill, society trusts you with the liberty to steal, the State trusts you with the liberty to murder."

Now if he had added, "and liquor furnishes you with the inclination," he would at least have put some truth into the entire statement.

But let's see—

"The State trusts you with the liberty to kill; society trusts you with the liberty to steal." Since when? Doesn't society distinctly prohibit killing and stealing? Doesn't it organise a police force to prevent men from killing and stealing?

Let this illustrious preacher of personal liberty try to kill or steal in the presence of a big six foot policeman and he'll find out what becomes of his grandiloquent statement that society trusts him with the liberty to kill and to steal.

He'll have his face punched and his head clubbed and he'll find himself landed in jail—if he insists upon exercising his personal liberty—and he'll remain there because he has proven that he is a dangerous citizen—too dangerous to exercise the personal liberty of which he boasts. No—God and society say very plainly regarding these and other matters—"*Thou shalt not*"—and this is plain prohibition.

As far as possible every reasonable measure is taken to prevent men from committing crime, and when they disobey the very reasonable laws which are framed for the safeguarding of men as a whole, they are punished by both God and society.

A Moral Question

There was a time when men honestly believed that they had a right to own slaves—because they thought it was purely a question of property rights—but today we know it is also a moral question.

There was a time when men honestly believed that all they needed to do to get a wife was to take a club and hit the woman of their choice on the head and drag her home, but today—well, women have something to say about it, too.

There was a time when men honestly believed that they had an absolute right to do with their children as they pleased, but today they recognise the fact that children have rights of their own.

Slaves, women, children—these have come to their own because a new conception of rights and duties has dawned upon men. They discovered that there is a more fundamental question than property rights—that duty is a bigger word than rights.

And so the weaker members of society are today being given a better chance.

But we still hark back to the property rights period and the question of personal liberty when we discuss the saloon and the liquor business. We forget that the biggest thing in this discussion is duty and sacrifice—for the sake of the weaker members of society—and we should be ready to give up our rights when the well-being of mankind as a whole is concerned.

The man who is ready to do this proves that he is a big man—the little man always stands out for his rights no matter what happens.

"Prohibition is based upon the idea that you can take away one man's liberty because of another man's act. The Drys want to run society on the principle of an insane asylum. Is that sound? They find a sick man and they want to compel everybody to take medicine. They find a man with a crutch and they try to compel every man to carry a crutch all his life," recently said one of the chief exponents of the liquor business.

He's wrong. The "Drys" do not want to run society on the principle of an insane asylum; they are so dead set against insane asylums that they don't want anybody to go there— particularly on account of the influence of liquor; and they don't want to compel everybody to take medicine—they want to eliminate the cause of disease so that nobody will have to take medicine.

They don't want to compel every man to carry a crutch all his life—they want to abolish the evil which compels men to walk on crutches. They don't want to take away anybody's liberty, because, as Blackstone[2] says, "Laws when prudently framed are by no means subversive but rather introductive of liberty.". . .

The First Consideration Is Society

In law and in civilisation the first consideration is not the individual, but society. Therefore, whatever injures society is not permitted. The greater our civilisation, the more restricted become our liberties. You may enjoy civic liberty only as you are willing to sacrifice personal liberty.

This does not mean that you are actually surrendering anything. Each of us is asked to give up some little things

2. Sir William Blackstone (1723–1780), English jurist and professor whose writings influenced common law in early America

and put them into the common fund which makes up the sum of all our comforts in a civilised community, but each of us draws out of that common fund much more than any of us puts in.

You may exercise your personal liberty only insofar as you do not place additional burdens upon your neighbours, or upon the State.

No man has a right to drink if by so doing he poisons himself or makes himself an unfit member of society, compelling the State to cure him, support him when he is unable to take care of himself, lock him up when he is dangerous to be at large, bury him at public expense when he is a corpse, and take care of his family after he is gone.

No normal man would prefer to live in a state of barbarism where every one does absolutely as he pleases without regard to the well-being of his neighbours. He would rather make some sacrifices which mean comparatively little to him in order that he, too, might make a contribution to the civilisation which is bringing so much happiness and comfort to all.

When a man thinks there is no other place under God's heaven in which he can drink liquor except in the saloon, and if he insists upon exercising his personal liberty in order to carry out his desires, he is asking thousands of men and women to make a greater sacrifice and to suffer infinitely more because the saloon is licensed, than he would suffer or sacrifice were he to give up his right to patronize the saloon. . . .

Every Member of a Society Sacrifices Some Liberty

It is much easier for six people to live together in peace than it is for six hundred to live in harmony. But there are 100 million of us in this country, and each of us thinks that he is just as good as the other fellow, if not a little better. Suppose each of us tried to do just as we pleased? It would create a hopeless situation.

Justinian has reduced the whole doctrine of law to these

principles: "That we should live honestly, should hurt nobody, and should render to every one his due."

If these principles were applied to the liquor business, and all that goes with it, there would be no room for it. Blackstone, the great authority of law, says: "If man were to live in a state of nature unconnected with other individuals, there would be no occasion for any other law than the law of nature and the law of God. Neither could any other law possibly exist, for a law always supposes some superior who is to make it, and in a state of nature we are all equal without any other superior but Him who is the author of our being. But man was formed for society and, as is demonstrated by the writers on the subject, is neither capable of living alone nor indeed has the courage to do it. The community should guard the rights of each individual member, and in return for this protection each individual should submit to the law of the community, without which submission of all it is impossible that protection should be extended to any."

Blackstone further says: "Every man when he enters into society gives up a part of his natural liberty, as the price of so valuable a purchase; and, in consideration of receiving the advantages of mutual commerce, obliges himself to conform to those laws which the community has thought proper to establish. And this species of legal obedience and conformity is infinitely more desirable than that wild and savage liberty which is sacrificed to obtain it. For no man, who considers a moment, would wish to retain the absolute and uncontrolled power of doing whatever he pleases; the consequence of which is, that every other man also have the same power and then there would be no security to individuals in any of the enjoyments of life.

"Hence we may collect that the law, which restrains a man from doing mischief to his fellow-citizens, though it diminishes the natural, increases the civil liberty of mankind. Laws when prudently framed are by no means subversive, but rather introductive of liberty, for as Mr. Locke[3] has well ob-

---

3. English philosopher John Locke (1632–1700)

served, where there is no law there is no freedom. The constitution or frame of government, while it leaves the individual the entire master of his own conduct, nevertheless restricts or restrains him whenever the public's good is affected."

Prohibition for the Common Good

According to Blackstone, a man's personal liberty is restricted by certain great fundamental facts. For example, he points out that life is the immediate gift of God. Therefore, this life cannot be taken away, that is, it cannot be destroyed, not even by the person himself, nor by any other of his fellow creatures merely upon their own authority. Hence, the State has a right to preserve a man's health from such practices as may prejudice or annoy it. If, therefore, any institution or custom in the community has a tendency to destroy life or health, the State has a right to abolish such institution or custom.

When the manufacture of liquor makes life more burdensome to all the people, and when it creates social and economic problems which threaten to destroy the finest things in human life; when it destroys men's bodies and souls and becomes a menace to society, then we have a right to destroy the liquor traffic—even though it may cause some inconvenience to a comparatively few people who insist upon exercising their personal liberty.

We accept this principle in every other relationship in life—why not accept it with regard to the liquor business?

Alcoholism Is Obsolete in the Industrial Age

Ernest H. Cherrington

Early American settlers had daily practical uses for alcohol. It was consumed before a hard day's work to give a boost of energy or to brace a body against a winter chill. It was often safer than water to drink. In the modern age, however, Ernest H. Cherrington, manager of the Anti-Saloon League's publishing division, believed alcohol was no longer needed. He believed that alcohol, if anything, was more of a detriment in an industrialized and commercial age. The slower working pace on early farms did not require the lucidity and precision that operating modern technical equipment required. This article was printed in the *Anti-Saloon League Yearbook*, one of many publications put out by the American Issue Publishing Company. Cherrington believed the Anti-Saloon League's best weapon was the printed word, and his division produced more than forty tons of printed material a month.

This, in a special sense, is an industrial and commercial age. The implications, therefore, in the transformation which has taken place during the industrial revolution of the past few years deserve thoughtful consideration.

Railroad Prohibition

A few years ago, comparatively speaking, it was not unusual for newspapers to ascribe railroad wrecks to "drunken engi-

Excerpted from "Alcoholism Obsolete in Modern Industry," by Ernest H. Cherrington, *Anti-Saloon League Yearbook*, 1922.

neers." Railroad lines in America have increased in fifty years from fifty-three thousand miles to two hundred and sixty-four thousand miles. Railroad development of every character has gone forward in America; until today twenty billions of dollars are invested and two million men are employed at an annual compensation of three billion dollars. These railroads carry annually more than two thousand million tons of freight and more than one thousand million passengers. Yet with sixty thousand railroad locomotives being driven on all lines throughout America, how many wrecks are today charged to drunken engineers, or drunken train dispatchers? American railroads will not employ an engineer who uses intoxicants either on or off duty. This imperative railroad law carries a far greater degree of punishment than any local, state or national prohibitory law. Even the liquor interests in America have long since ceased to defend the personal liberty of railroad engineers to drink intoxicants.

When American railroads modify their rules which have stood for a quarter of a century, so as to permit engineers, train dispatchers, and telegraph operators to use light wines and beer, the American Congress will doubtless be ready seriously to consider the advisability of modifying the Federal prohibition law.

Iron and Steel Versus Alcoholism

The giant lake freighters, which carry ore from the great Superior ore districts, are unloaded at American lake ports whence the ore is transported by trains to the numerous smelting furnaces of the United States, which produce more iron and steel each year than all the rest of the world. Comparatively a few years ago, vessels were unloaded by laborers with shovels and wheelbarrows. The unloading capacity under the old system was a hundred tons a day. Today electric machines load such vessels at the rate of three thousand tons an hour. Even greater revolutions than this have taken place in the electrical equipment of iron and steel mills.

Under the old system it was possible for an unskilled employee with a brain well soaked with alcohol, to handle a shovel and a wheelbarrow. The intricate modern unloading equipment, however, cannot be entrusted to habitual users of alcoholic liquors. The same rule applies with even greater force to the vast electrical equipment now operating the iron and steel mills of the nation. When the iron and steel industry of America advocates the letting down of prohibition bars, Congress may heed the suggestion.

Dealcoholizing the Mining Industry

During the last ten years modern electrical inventions revolutionized the American coal mining industry. Electrical mining machines with two operators today do the work which a decade ago required twenty miners. Seven hundred and fifty thousand American miners who already are producing more than 40 per cent of all the coal used in all the countries of the world, cannot begin to meet the demands even with the installation of modern equipment. Under the old system a miner with a brain fairly well soaked with alcohol could produce a few tons of coal a day, but the man who operates a modern electric mining machine must be sober.

The Passing of the "Drunken Sailor"

During the past nine years the tonnage of American ships clearing American ports increased from 4,793,523 net tons to 30,180,809 net tons—an increase of more than 500 per cent. The modern system of electric devices for the handling of ship cargoes installed on ships and at docks during the last few years has not only eliminated the proverbial "drunken sailor," but has created an imperative requirement for skilled men with clear brains. The old drunken sailor cannot meet the new test. America's part in the international commerce of the future cannot be jeopardized by compromise with the old system under which alcohol played a leading role.

An Industrial Revolution

Perhaps no series of legislative acts have so aroused the manufacturing interests in America to the absolute necessity of prohibition as the workmen's compensation laws passed during recent years in all but three states of the American Union. As a result, millions upon millions have been invested in safety devices for the protection of life, limb and health of the ten million American manufacturing employees. Safety to workers and insurance to manufacturing interests preclude the possibility of those interests accepting the hazard which would be inevitable with the return of the beverage liquor traffic.

The Auto Truck and the Old Teamster

Only a few years ago the vast tonnage of agricultural products and of industrial and commercial enterprises in America was moved on short hauls by wagons with teams and teamsters. Today the great proportion of that tonnage is moved by auto trucks. One large truck will move more tonnage than could be moved under the old system by ten wagons. Under the old system, half-drunken drivers might throw the lines around the dashboard and depend upon the dumb animals drawing the load to avoid collision and the ditch. But the intrinsic value of more than a million automobile trucks now operating in America, to say nothing of the value of the tonnage involved, cannot be entrusted to alcoholized truck drivers.

An Automobilized Nation Without Prohibition

There are in operation in America ten million automobiles. All the rest of the world together employs two million automobiles. America therefore may be said to be the most thoroughly automobilized nation in the world. The great development of the automobile industry has taken place in the last decade, during which same period prohibition by state legislation was rapidly covering the area of the nation. The beverage alcohol system in operation in automobilized America today is unthinkable. What degree of safety, under alcohol, could be vouchsafed to any traveler upon any highway or any pedestrian upon any sidewalk of any town or any city? If America faces such a situation now, what will other countries of the world do in regard to this important question, as the use of automobiles rapidly increases?

Insurance Risks and Prohibition Inseparable

Perhaps no department of American business has developed so rapidly as life insurance. Insurance estates are rapidly becoming important factors in the financial world. In slightly more than thirty years the amount of life insurance in America has increased from five billion dollars to more than forty-two billion dollars. The number of life insurance policies in existence in the United States in 1890 was 5,202,475. The number in 1900 was 14,395,347. The number in 1910 was 29,998,281, while the number in 1920 was 64,341,000. Investigations of actuaries covering long periods have established a decided difference between the actual costs of risks on the lives of abstainers as against those of non-abstainers. With this remarkable increase in the number and amount of risks carried by the American insurance companies, the greater part of which increase has come during the period of state and national prohibition, even the suggestion of a return to the days of alcoholism is startling. What would happen to millions of insurance risks, to the insurance companies themselves, and to the vast financial interests of America, in which those insurance companies now play so significant a part, were the beverage liquor traffic to be restored, with its attendant results through the use of alcohol, upon millions of policy holders, and its even more far-reaching effect upon mortality statistics that would inevitably result from accidents, disease and crime that would follow like an avalanche in the wake of alcoholism?

Aeronautics Demand Sobriety

The airship is in its infancy, yet the development of the past five years is prophetic of a day not many years ahead when the airship will be one of the most important factors in the life of the world. Leaving out of consideration all government, army and navy airship activities, the fact remains that during the year 1921 more than twelve hundred civilian aeroplanes were operated in America, traveling more than six million five hundred thousand miles and carrying more than two hundred and seventy-five thousand passengers. It is not rash to prophesy that the airship in ten year's time will work a revolution in industry, commerce, travel, international relations and international law. Development of the airship as a real agency of travel and commerce in America under conditions which would be inevitable with the return of the beverage liquor traffic, is out of the question.

Alcoholism an Impossibility in the New Age

The liquor traffic may have been possible in the agricultural world in the age of the horse-drawn plow and the mule teamster; it is not possible in the age of the tractor, the great wheat-header and the auto truck. The liquor traffic may have been possible in the days when the wood chopper's ax was the only means of felling trees; it is not possible in the age when electrical operations are so essential to the rapidly increasing lumber industry. The liquor traffic may have been possible in the age of the drunken sailor and the drunken engineer and the age when manufacturing concerns were not responsible for the health and safety of employees; it is not possible in the age of the industrial development which has revolutionized railroad operations, the mining industry, manufacturing interests, international commerce and trade activities, and other great industries and enterprises which figure in economic progress. The liquor traffic may have been possible in the age of the ox-cart, but it is not possible in the age of the automobile. The liquor traffic may have been possible in the age of the stage coach, but it is not possible in the age of the airship. The liquor traffic may have been possible in the age of the water mill, but it is not possible in the age of the electric dynamo.

Liquor Has Always Been in League with Rebellion

Wayne B. Wheeler

Wayne B. Wheeler was a spokesman for the Ohio-based Anti-Saloon League. He was one of the most powerful figures in the Prohibition movement and helped draft the Eighteenth Amendment and the Volstead Act. Wheeler had a terrible alcohol-related accident as a child, so his hatred for alcohol was intense. He was not afraid to use any means possible to further his organization's Prohibition aims. The following 1921 article is Wheeler's unabashed response to the dry propagandists' claim that Prohibition was unconstitutional and un-American. He cites historical examples of the liquor industry's insurrectionist tradition of defying the law. Wheeler even exploits the insecurities left by World War I by questioning the loyalty of German American brewery owners.

A rebellion is an organized attempt to forcibly resist the government. A rum rebellion is an attempt of the liquor interests to nullify the Constitution, or the laws, or to defy them, instead of changing them by the orderly processes of government. Liquor is now and always has been in rebellion against government control.

The first historic rum rebellion, commonly called The Whisky Rebellion of western Pennsylvania, occurred in 1794. Distilling whisky was the chief industry of that sec-

Excerpted from "Rum Rebellions Past and Present," by Wayne B. Wheeler, *Forum*, May 1921.

tion. The price of the finished product was a shilling a gallon, and the tax proposed was seven cents a gallon. The whisky dealers rebelled at the imposition of the tax. They declared it was an interference with a legitimate business and an infringement upon their personal liberty. Those who counselled obedience to the law were visited with gross insults. Officers were assaulted; many people were killed. An attempt was made by the liquor dealers to call out the militia in their behalf, so as to involve so many in the crime of resistance that the government would not attempt to punish the insurrection. A number of people in Pittsburgh incurred the displeasure of the whisky dealers because they counselled obedience to the law, and the city was threatened with destruction. The governor failed to meet the situation promptly and President Washington made a requisition of thirteen thousand militia from Pennsylvania and adjoining states to suppress the rebellion. When the whisky insurgents realized that the government was in earnest, they capitulated, and two of the leaders were tried and convicted of treason.

Many of the families involved in the affair left the section and settled in the mountains of Kentucky, and the names of some famous moonshiners in Kentucky today are the same as those of certain leaders of the Pennsylvania Whisky Rebellion.

A History of Defiance

The attitude of liquor toward law has always been one of rebellion. The liquor traffic has defied every regulative, restrictive and prohibitory law placed on the statute books, and the present open rebellion of the traffic against the Constitution of the United States is only the final step in its long fight against the orderly processes of government.

During the War of 1812, when the government felt the necessity of increasing its revenue to sustain it in the extra burdens it was obliged to carry, a small tax in comparison to that which is now borne by the traffic, was laid upon the liquor trade. At the close of the war, the liquor dealers compelled Congress to remove this excise tax which had been levied to support the War of 1812. The inside historic facts concerning the repeal of the tax reflect no credit upon the methods used by the trade to secure immunity.

The unpatriotic attitude of the liquor traffic was revealed during the days of the Civil War. When the government was torn and bleeding at every pore, and the trade knew that the nation required money in order to continue the struggle, it reversed its attitude taken at the close of the War of 1812, and made a seductive plea for increased taxation on the trade. Prohibition sentiment had been increasing, and the trade knew that the best way to buy continuance of life was by paying what was then considered a liberal license. When once this policy was fastened on the government the liquor dealers realized the advantage it gave them, and they have since used it as their chief weapon against prohibition. Lincoln knew the danger that would lie in the liquor revenue, and he foresaw how it would dull the conscience of the people, therefore he signed the bill that brought it with great reluctance, and only with the understanding that the measure would be repealed after the war.

When the smoke had lifted from the battle fields, and when the din of battle had subsided into the sobs and moans of war-made widows and orphans, it was found that the liquor traffic had entrenched itself in the state and Federal revenue laws, and had repealed state prohibitory laws save those of Maine alone. The good work of half a century done by earnest temperance folk had been undone.

The present slogan of the wets, "Prohibition was put over" has in it not a ghost of truth, but had the drys cried for the past fifty years "the liquor traffic was put over while the country bled for freedom and for unity in the Civil War," they would have had the facts on their side.

True to its colors the liquor traffic created scandal in army operations in Cuba and the Philippines, and in the army camps during the Spanish-American War the canteen outrage was its contribution toward promoting the morale of our troops.

The same demoralizing and degrading forces that had

played traitor during the Civil War were at work to disrupt our army, and another chapter in the story of the Rum Rebellion was written in our national history.

Curbs, checks, regulations have been continuously ignored by the liquor traffic. It has persistently refused to obey the excise laws in New York, Chicago, San Francisco, and in practically all of the large cities, until public sentiment compelled their enforcement or until it was prohibited. It has always been a notorious fact that saloons have refused to obey the Sunday closing law. It has been the proud boast of many of their owners that they threw away their door keys when they opened their establishments. Municipal scandals have grown out of the fact that corrupt politicians and their official pawns, mayors and police heads, have refused to enforce Sunday closing laws, while the laws against selling to minors and intoxicated persons were brazenly ignored in the past.

Anti-American Affiliations

The attitude of the liquor interests during the World War was characteristic. The government appealed to the people to save food, fuel and transportation facilities to win the war. The liquor interests continued to waste food by the ton, while the people saved it by the pound. They used the cars and the coal needed to send food and supplies to the front to ship their beer and debauch the people, when the country, nay the world, needed a sober manhood and womanhood with all faculties and powers intact. They allied themselves with the disloyal forces in the government. The German-American Alliance secured a charter from the Federal government. Its activities, however, put it under suspicion and the government investigated. The testimony given before the Senate Judiciary Committee showed that this organization was disloyal, and it was also proved that the United States Brewers' Association, and brewers known to be pro-German, furnished much money used for German propaganda as well as for propaganda against prohibition.

The representative of the brewers on the witness stand admitted that the National Association of Commerce and Labor, interested primarily in combatting prohibition, was to operate through the German-American Alliance, with the consent of the president and vice-president of the Alliance, and that the funds for the propaganda emanated in reality from the United States Brewers' Association.

The German-American Alliance Charter was revoked by the Congress without a dissenting vote. Following this the United States Senate ordered an investigation of the entire corrupt practices of the brewers and of their political activities. Over seven thousand pages of sworn testimony were taken. The committee found every one of the charges in Senate Resolution 307 were substantially sustained:

> That the said United States Brewers' Association, brewing companies, and allied interests have in recent years made contributions to political campaigns on a great scale without precedent in the political history of the country and in violation of the laws of the land;

> That in order to control legislation in the State and Nation, they have exacted pledges from candidates to office, including Congressmen and United States Senators, before election, such pledges being on file;

> That, in order to influence public opinion to their ends, they have heavily subsidized the public press and stipulated when contracting for advertising space with the newspapers that a certain amount be editorial space, the literary material for the space being provided from the brewers' central office in New York;

> That, in order to suppress expressions of opinion hostile to their trade and political interests, they have set in operation an extensive system of boycotting of American manufacturers, merchants, railroads, and other interests;

> That for the furthering of their political enterprises, they have erected a political organization to carry out their purposes;

> That they were allied to powerful suborganizations, among them the German-American Alliance, whose charter was revoked by the unanimous vote of Congress; the National Association at Com-

merce and Labor; and the Manufacturers and Dealers' Associations; and that they have their ramifications in other organizations neutral in character;

That they have on file political surveys of states, counties and districts tabulating the men and forces for and against them, and that they have paid large sums of money to citizens of the United States to advocate their cause and interests, including some in the government employ;

That they have defrauded the Federal Government by applying to their political corruption funds money which should have gone to the Federal Treasury in taxes.

The Liquor Industry Is Opportunistic and Disloyal

Step by step we have shown the rebelliousness and disloyalty of the now outlawed liquor traffic up to the adoption of Federal prohibition. It defied the government in 1794; it was a tax-dodger in 1812; it took advantage of its country's necessity in the Civil War to entrench itself in public life; in the Spanish-American War it debauched our troops; in the World War it was pro-German and anti-American. Is it not logical that today it should be in open rebellion against the Constitution of the United States and should incite to lawlessness and encourage nullification?

When two-thirds of Congress submitted the Eighteenth Amendment and fifteen-sixteenths of the states ratified it, people who had not studied the history of the liquor traffic thought the liquor interests would submit and obey the law until it was changed in a legal and orderly manner. Instead of doing this, the nine national liquor organizations continued their work against prohibition, and five new national liquor organizations came into the field to help.

"The Association Opposed to National Prohibition" has its headquarters in New York. It has boasted that it had $1,000,000,000 subscribed to see to it that the Eighteenth Amendment should not become operative. The "Association Opposed to the Prohibition Amendment" has its headquarters in Washington. It boasts that no liquor dealer is eligible, but its program is as follows, according to its own statement:

1. To get the Volstead Act out of the law.
2. To permit every state under the concurrent clause to pass its own enforcement act.

It also states in a paragraph of its prospectus: "If the majority of voters do not favor the law and if those against it organize so that they may be counted, the law will be repealed and the regulatory power under the prohibition amendment will be left to each state under the concurrent clause." The acknowledged program of these two organizations is simply a defiance of the Eighteenth Amendment. The New York organization frankly admits that its purpose is to prevent the Eighteenth Amendment from becoming operative.

The Washington organization proposes to repeal the Volstead Act and thus allow the wet states to remain wet in spite of the Constitution, and the dry states to enact and enforce their own laws. No one can gainsay the fact that this means rebellion against national prohibition as written into the Constitution of the United States.

The campaign to overthrow the Eighteenth Amendment by other than legal methods is as follows:

The Association Opposed to National Prohibition planned to create a public sentiment by a false propaganda that would coerce the Supreme Court into a decision in their favor. . . .

It planned to elect a Congress to repeal or destroy the laws to make the Eighteenth Amendment enforceable. This is legislative rebellion.

It planned to elect public officials, bound by duty to enforce the law, who would encourage law-breakers in their lawlessness.

Governor [Edward L.] Edwards [of New Jersey, 1920–1923], backed by the liquor interests, determined to capture the national convention of his own party in the interest of outlawed liquor and to make his own state as wet as the Atlantic Ocean. Fortunately, he met his Waterloo, and New Jersey is now again in the Union.

The Prosecuting Attorney at Iron River, Michigan, headed

a rebellion against the Federal officers who seized liquor in that community. In the name of the law, this officer of the law attempted to discredit faithful Federal officers. The legality of the seizure of the liquor in question was decided in the Federal court upholding the Federal officers, and this rebellion, too, was nipped in the bud.

Chicago wets joined the rum rebellion, and would have succeeded in part, because of the indifference of the city administration, and the United States District Attorney who refused to do his duty; but faithful Federal enforcement officials, and the courageous Attorney General of Illinois, Mr. Brundage, have curbed the law-breakers even with the odds against them.

San Francisco's liquor hosts rebelled, and its wet mayor boasted of the ready flow of liquor during the Democratic National Convention. The rebellious liquor traffic corrupted a number of Federal enforcement officials. The Federal Enforcement Department has taken drastic measures to reorganize the forces and suppress the rebellion at the Golden Gate.

New York, in her liquor delirium, not only defied the law, but became the headquarters of forged permits and bribed Federal inspectors and agents. Practically all of the Federal appointees for the enforcement of prohibition in New York had to be discharged. A new force is now at work, and time will tell whether its members can stand the test of liquor bribes.

Milwaukee naturally takes part in the rum rebellion. A recent Federal Grand Jury in this district took occasion to use its official position to become propagandists for the outlawed liquor interests and applied to Congress to repeal the Law Enforcement Code.

Parts of Pennsylvania, true to the spirit of 1794, are in rebellion against the enforcement of any Federal law prohibiting the liquor traffic. Pennsylvania, New York, Rhode Island, Connecticut, and New Jersey have vied with each other in their liquor lawlessness for years. They represent the black belt of the liquor rebellion. The present outlook, however, for the passage of state enforcement codes in four of these commonwealths is hopeful. With their passage will come the dawn of a new era for law and order.

A band of unscrupulous patent and proprietary medicine manufacturers and venders are joining the rebellion, with the cloak of respectability wrapped about them. A relentless warfare is being carried on against these substitutes for booze.

Aiding Insurrection

Public officers who take an oath of office to support the Constitution and enforce laws enacted pursuant thereto, and then make the enforcement of the law a mockery by their indifference and their public utterances, and a farce by inadequate fines, are particeps criminis [an accessory to the crime] to the rebellion.

Politicians who use their influence to secure illegal permits to withdraw liquor are guilty of aiding the rebellion.

Those sleek money-grabbers who quietly manage the bootleg and forged permit system, who bribe officers and subsidize press agents to condemn the law, are the chief criminals in the rebellion. They should be singled out for special punishment, and if there is a place on earth willing to receive such traitors they should be deported.

Newspapers and magazines that become propagandists for law-breakers and encourage defiance of law, are aiders and abettors of the insurrection. There is a place always in this nation for those opposed to any law who are ready to use legal methods to repeal it, but there is no place under the Stars and Stripes for those who defy the law and encourage anarchy.

Mr. William Jennings Bryan [former Congressman and three-time presidential nominee who fought repeal] has paid his compliments to those so-called American citizens who go to Cuba, Bimini, the Bahamas, and other foreign territory, and use it as a base for defying the laws of their country, in this characteristic language:

> Statistics show that British territory on the north and just off the east coast of the United States is being used as a base for the wholesale smuggling of intoxicating liquors in this country. There

is no more excuse for the use of the adjacent territory for conspiracies against the Prohibition law—a law carrying out the Constitution and sustained by the Supreme Court—than for the use of such territory for conspiracies against any other law of the land. Piracy would not be given protection under the British flag. Why should smuggling?

The easiest way to punish such citizens is to withdraw citizenship from them when they leave the country for the purpose of violating their country's laws. If they violate the laws while in this country they can be punished as criminals. Why should they receive the protection of their government while conspiring against their country's statutes? If they leave for that purpose, or while away become law-breakers, their return should be barred as we bar the entrance of any other criminal.

The Rebellion Must Be Ended

No government can live if it permits a rebellion to continue within its borders. A rum rebellion is as bad or worse than any other rebellion. Those who participate in it not only menace the fundamental principles of government, but they fight for a cause which debauches and demoralizes the citizenship of the Republic. Any citizen or group of citizens, or public officials who defy the law must be regarded as public enemies. No one in a democracy has any excuse for rebelling against the law because it interferes with his personal habits. In a monarchy those who defy the laws, even though they have no part in making them, are summarily dealt with. In a democracy, where every citizen has his chance to help frame the laws by majority rule, and can work for their repeal if so inclined, the obligation of loyalty and obedience to law is infinitely greater even than in a monarchy.

Rebellions must be suppressed—by force if necessary. Force, however, will not be necessary in order to suppress the rum rebellion because an increasing number of those who oppose prohibition agree that it should be enforced until it is repealed in an orderly manner. But the drys are confident that each year of enforced prohibition will prove its benefits to the people so that the opposition will gradually die out.

It is to be hoped that the government will not only continue and increase its activity to enforce the law, but also give its encouragement to a great patriotic campaign to create a larger respect for law. Obedience to law needs more emphasis at this time. This is a legitimate governmental function. Unless law is respected and enforced, the government itself must fail. All of our personal and property rights are dependent upon the honest enforcement of law. Lincoln well said: "To violate the law is to tear the charter of your own and your children's liberty." Obedience to law is liberty. Violation of law is anarchy. This nation must choose which course it will follow.

Chapter 2

The Wets

Chapter Preface

D espite the seemingly overwhelming support of national prohibition by the public and lawmakers during the 1920s, the Eighteenth Amendment had many opponents, even among supporters of temperance. Many politicians, including President Woodrow Wilson and former secretary of state Elihu Root, opposed the Eighteenth Amendment because of its unconstitutionality. Other "wet" groups, including the Association Against the Prohibition Amendment (AAPA), saw Prohibition as a threat to public policy. They believed the law wrongly expanded the role of federal government by granting them power to regulate individual behavior. They also believed the government's inability to enforce Prohibition laws was generating public disdain for the government.

One of the ironies of the anti-Prohibition movement was that its largest support came from women. Women's political activism had mainly been associated with the temperance movement, but just as many women fought against Prohibition. To their constituents, both pro- and anti-alcohol movements were liberating: The Prohibition campaign had given women their first taste of political power, and the illicit and underground life of speakeasies during the ban had given other women social acceptance in formerly male dominated realms.

The Woman's Organization for National Prohibition Reform was one of the most influential prorepeal organizations that united hundreds of thousands of women across the country. The WONPR adopted the propaganda and political pressure techniques of the dry forces, as well as taking the battle to the doorsteps of homes all over the country. Members canvassed from house to house and were able to pick up victories in heavily conservative towns and states by taking a personal approach. The WONPR also launched a letter writing campaign to members of Congress, whom they urged to adopt a wet platform. They were able to sway many supporters since the size and influence of the WONPR had grown so quickly. The WONPR followed up with a massive effort, including newspaper and radio campaigns, to get out the vote. Eventually their efforts were rewarded when victories were announced in state after state. The WONPR disbanded after repeal was clinched. The organization had not only succeeded in bringing about repeal, it had also shown the nation that women were capable of acting as effective political leaders.

Prohibition Is the Devil's Deceit

Joseph F. Rutherford

The temperance movement was founded and promoted by Christians, but not all Christians supported Prohibition. Judge Joseph F. Rutherford, the second president of the Watchtower Bible and Tract Society (which became known as Jehovah's Witnesses in 1931), ardently opposed the Eighteenth Amendment. Rutherford, despite being a heavy drinker, supported temperance in theory. It was the hypocrisy of the dry prohibitionists that infuriated him. In an article that appeared in a 1924 issue of his organization's official publication, *The Watchtower*, Rutherford explains how prohibitionists have been deceived. Rutherford believed any law that inspired that kind of deceit in decent people was a scheme concocted by the devil. This statement drew a lot of protest from some other religious organizations that already considered the Watchtower Society as heretical.

S ince the time of Abel there have been some good men who desire to eliminate evil from the earth. Various methods have been employed to this end and all without success. The Jews tried the method of keeping the Law, and were not able to keep either the spirit or the letter thereof. Some have tried to make themselves righteous, but have learned that such is impossible. Others have been trying to eliminate evil by legislation. This method also has failed.

God is not limited in power. He could destroy evil at any

Excerpted from "Prohibition," by Joseph F. Rutherford, *The Watchtower*, November 1, 1924.

time. He has permitted it for some good reason. The fact that he has permitted it and has not destroyed it is a sufficient reason for Christians not to attempt to run ahead of the Lord in its elimination. One of the reasons, which seems apparent, is to give all intelligent creatures a full opportunity to acknowledge, accept, and serve Jehovah as God or to follow the way of the devil; in other words to give an opportunity to prove man's loyalty to his Creator. God has permitted man to have experience with evil, that he might learn lasting lessons; and when the time comes for God to establish righteousness in the earth, those who learn the lessons as he has arranged them will become righteous. The great Creator has made man a free moral agent, placed good and evil before him, and given him the choice of selecting one and rejecting the other.

The real issue before man is God or the devil. God has a well-defined plan concerning man, which plan will successfully eliminate all evil from the earth. Every part of the divine plan Satan, the mimic god, has tried to copy. The devil's counterfeit plan has been for the purpose of deceiving mankind, making God appear a liar, and his Word untrustworthy. Up to this time Satan has succeeded well in blinding the people.

We have now come to a crisis in the affairs of man. Legally the devil's dominion is at an end. The rightful King, the beloved Son of God, is here and has taken his sovereign power. Satan desires to hold the people in subjection to himself. Hence it must be expected that he will resort to every possible means of fraud and deceit to accomplish his end.

The Duty of the Christian

What is the duty of each Christian under the circumstances? We answer: His duty is plain. Having entered into a covenant with God by sacrifice through the merit of Christ Jesus, and having been begotten to the divine nature, he has solemnly agreed to do the will of God. Any other course willingly taken would be disloyalty to God, and therefore a repudiation of his covenant. There is no possible ground of compromise for the Christian. To be a Christian one must be on the Lord's side; and when he willingly ceases to be on the Lord's side, he ceases to be a Christian. Surely every true Christian will agree that these statements are sound and true.

Recently the President of our Association, responding to a question concerning the Eighteenth Amendment of the Constitution of the United States, which prohibits the manufacture, sale and transportation of intoxicating liquor within the United States and which is known as the prohibition law, said, "Prohibition is a scheme of the devil," referring of course to the law above mentioned. Some of the brethren have made strenuous protests against this statement. Because of the seeming misunderstanding we deem it proper for *The Watchtower* to state the Scriptural view of the matter.

In the outset it must be conceded by all fair-minded people that prohibition is either the result of God's will being done on earth or else a scheme of the devil. Let each one judge which it is in the light of the undisputed facts.

A desire to eliminate intoxicating liquor and all other evils is a proper and laudable desire. All Christians should be in accord with that desire. But how to accomplish that end is a different thing. The devil has a way of appearing to accomplish it, and his way is that of fraud and deceit.

God's way of accomplishing that end is righteous and complete. In his own due time he will completely eliminate intoxicating liquors and all other evil influences. He has said to man: "For as the heavens are higher than the earth, so are my ways higher than your ways, and my thoughts than your thoughts" (Isaiah 55:9).

God's way is not popular with the majority of mankind at present. All true Christians are for God's way. "He who seeks the approval of the world and who is a friend of the world is an enemy of God" (Jas. 4:4). The Lord's friendship and his approval are the only things worthwhile.

Intoxicating liquor is a great evil. The devil stands for all things evil. He is the very personification of wickedness. Then how could prohibition of intoxicating liquor be the devil's scheme? St. Paul answers: "For Satan himself is transformed into an angel of light. Therefore it is no great thing if his ministers also be transformed as the ministers of righteousness" (2 Cor. 11:14,15). In the prohibition scheme he appears as an angel of light; his ministers likewise. Fraud and deceit are Satan's principal methods of operation. He is the god of this evil world, and has long deceived the nations and blinded their minds to the truth of God's plan (1 Cor. 4:4).

Under the Influence of Satan

More than a century ago good men and women, seeing the evil of intoxicating liquor, started a movement to expel it from the earth. In America they organized the Prohibition Party. That party is now dead, and had nothing to do with the enactment of the Eighteenth Amendment. But even had that party succeeded in its plan, such would not have been God's way.

Long ago Satan caused the union of church and state in Europe, and therefore the downfall of the clergy. He desired to accomplish the same thing in America. Union of church and state is repugnant to the fundamental American principles. To accomplish his end Satan knew that he must resort to fraud and deceit by putting forth something that had the appearance of good. The World War furnished the opportunity for him to act, and he did act.

Jesus taught his followers to pray: "Thy kingdom come. Thy will be done on earth as it is in heaven," and also taught them to wait for his second coming for the setting up of that kingdom and the establishment of righteousness. Satan induced the clergy to believe that they could set up God's kingdom on earth without waiting for the Lord, and that to accomplish this they must bring into the church men of wealth, influence and power. The clergy fell under this temptation, brought in the profiteers, politicians and other men of influence, and made them the chief ones in their congregations. The ruling factors have long been under the influence of Satan, whether they knew it or not. The chief ones amongst the rulers are those of commercial power. It is a well-known fact in America that this power has nominated the candidates for the leading parties for several years, and has elected the one they desired.

The commercial powers were induced to see that if liquor could be taken away from the laboring man the result would be beneficial to bankers, manufacturers and merchants. Big business, the real controlling power of the politicians of the land under the super mind of their guiding and invisible god (Satan), set about to unite the forces of the Democratic and Republican parties to accomplish their purpose. It was an easy matter to get the preachers to do the shouting and to make the noise, because they felt that now big business and big politicians were with them and that they could set up the Lord's kingdom in earth. The World War furnished the opportunity, and an appeal was made to the people by the politicians and the preachers to patriotically support the movement for prohibition in order to win the war, and thus many were induced to support it.

The appeal was made to the order-loving ones by the preachers that it was the will of God that prohibition should be enacted; and the people were again deceived, and acted accordingly. By the combined action of big business, big politicians, and big preachers they induced the Congress to take the necessary steps to amend the Constitution, and the state legislatures to ratify it. At the time, the *New York Tribune* editorially said, "This legislation seems to be propelled by some invisible force." It was indeed an invisible force, and that force was the devil. The result was a union of clergy with big business and big politicians in a combination to control the American people.

Can any Christian, who believes God and his Word, for one moment think that the Lord God of righteousness used the Democratic and Republican parties, and the higher critics and evolutionists, and those who deny the blood of Christ Jesus, to enact the prohibition law; and that such was his will and plan? Does the God of righteousness need any such unholy alliance as this to accomplish his will on earth? Does any Christian believe that this is the plan of God? If not, then whose scheme is it?

Prohibition Is Not God's Way

It is well known that the ultra-rich, the politicians, and even many clergy are supplied with all the intoxicating liquor they can consume, while they are making the greatest noise for the enforcement of the prohibition law. As an illustration: One influential clergyman, who led the fight in his vicinity for prohibition, shortly after the enactment of the law had his house burglarized. The burglars found his cellar stocked with liquors, and indulged in same so freely that they broke up his furniture. The clergyman refused to prosecute the guilty ones because it would expose the fact that he, an advocate of prohibition, had stocked up well in advance, that he might not need to deny himself things that he was willing to take away from his neighbors merely for show.

It is also well known that many of the agencies employed to enforce the prohibition law have taken the illicit liquor away from the bootlegger and either used it themselves or sold it to others. Many of the prohibition law officers have connived with others to steal great quantities of liquor from warehouses, and have then wrongfully sold it to others or divided it amongst those particularly favored by them. Can any Christian for a moment believe that prohibition, as we now see it, is the result of God's will done on earth?

Intoxicating liquor is a great evil, and the saloons a curse to humanity. The good American people do not want either. They are also sick and disgusted with pious-faced frauds, who parade in the name of Christ, hypocritically claiming to be representing God and righteousness, who join hands with the conscienceless politicians and profiteers to enact and enforce a law, and claim it to be the carrying out of God's will. When Jesus was on earth he denounced above everything else fraud and hypocrisy. God's Word admonishes Christians to abstain from every form of evil. Fraud and hypocrisy are amongst the greatest evils.

Let the people adopt the Lord's way, accept Christ and his kingdom, and be submissive thereto; and their ways will be right. But so long as the people adopt Satan's fraudulent methods and ignore the Lord's way they can not accomplish a lasting good. All Christians should refuse to stultify themselves by joining hands with any scheme that has the appearance of good when in truth and in fact it is honeycombed with fraud and deceit, and denies the Lord and his methods of accomplishing the blessing of mankind.

No Christian advocates the use of intoxicating liquor. The question is not concerning the existence of the evil, but the *method* of elimination of that evil. Instead of running ahead of the Lord and joining hands with some scheme that is contrary to the Lord's way, the Christian should remember the scripture: "Be patient therefore, brethren, unto the coming of the Lord. Behold, the husbandman waiteth for the precious fruit of the earth, and hath long patience for it, until he receive the early and latter rain. Be ye also patient; establish your hearts; for the coming of the Lord draweth nigh. Take, my brethren, the prophets, who have spoken in the name of the Lord, for an example of suffering affliction, and of patience" (James 5:7,8,10).

Reformation Impossible by Legislation

The Lord Jesus is now present. His kingdom is at hand. Satan, in his desperation to deceive the people, has appeared as an angel of light and has put forth a thing, to wit, prohibition, which appears to be good but which in truth and in fact is a fraudulent scheme to turn the minds of the people away from Christ and his kingdom. God, in his own due time, will eliminate intoxicating liquor and all other evils from the earth; and when he does so, there will be no apostate preachers ("Ministers of Satan appearing as ministers of righteousness"), no politicians and no profiteers advocating prohibition that their own selfish ends may be accomplished. There will be no fraudulent agencies claiming to enforce the law, and at the same time violating it. Shortly Satan will be shorn of his power (Rev. 20:1–4). The eyes of the people will be opened to the truth. The Lord will rule them in righteousness. He will have no dishonest agencies representing him; but, as he says, "when thy judgments [the

Lord's] are in the earth, the inhabitants of the world will learn righteousness" (Isa. 26:9).

Experience shows that it is impossible to reform men of evil merely by legislation. This does not mean that men should not be reformed, but when the great Jehovah God has plainly told us in his Word how these reformations will be brought about, every Christian should adopt the Lord's way because it is right and every Christian should refrain from the devil's way because it is wrong (2 Cor. 6:15–18).

The Christian would be more popular with the world to advocate the present scheme of prohibition. It is better to be right than to be popular. The Christian's allegiance must be to God and his kingdom. Remember the issue now is, The Lord's kingdom against Satan's rule. If we are followers of the Lord, then let us hear and obey his Word: "Wait yet upon me, saith the Lord . . . For then will I turn to the people a pure language, that they may all call upon the name of the Lord, to serve him with one consent" (Zeph. 3:8,9).

The Lord could prohibit intoxicating liquors at any time, but it is not yet his due time. It follows, then, that the scheme put forth at this particular time in the light of the evidence is not God's plan or scheme but that of the devil. In God's due time his kingdom will rule the nations and enforce righteousness. He will so reform the hearts of men that they will refrain from evil. For a Christian to be loyal to the Lord he must now stand for the Lord's way, and not for any other.

With the kindliest feeling toward all who desire the elimination of every form of evil from the earth, as Christians we must follow the Lord's way and wait upon him. The evidences are so conclusive at this time that his kingdom is at hand that there can be no doubt in the mind of one who is really informed on the Bible. Let each believer in the Bible then ask himself: Has God brought about the present condition of prohibition? If not, then should I advocate it? Is God going to reform through Christ's kingdom the world and eliminate evil and bring blessings to the people? If so, then I must be on the Lord's side.

The Watchtower has nothing to do with politics. Prohibition is not a political question. If the people of the world wish to make a prohibition law and enforce that law, well and good. That is not our affair. A Christian can not consistently participate therein. He must keep himself separate from the world. The sole question is, Who is on the Lord's side? If we are on the Lord's side, our way is clear: Be patient and wait upon him to fully establish his rule in the earth.

The Puritanical Foundations of the Prohibition Movement

Clarence Darrow

Prohibitionists considered alcohol to be the source of most of the major problems that plagued society. If drinking were abolished, they believed, crime, sickness, and poverty would disappear with it. They even went as far as hiring a scholar to rewrite the Bible and take all references to alcohol out. But anti-prohibitionists opposed the idea of limiting personal freedom in any way. They believed taking away the public's right to drink what they wanted would make it easier to limit other freedoms.

Defense attorney Clarence Darrow was not much of a drinker—which made him a good spokesman for the "wets"—but he considered Prohibition to be criminal. In his autobiography, *The Story of My Life,* Darrow regards Prohibition as a serious threat to the American way of life. He attacks the religious members of the Prohibition movement and cites their history of repressing individual liberties. These are the same opponents Darrow has faced in past trials and his writings reflect a cautious familiarity.

Clarence Darrow has been hailed as one of the most brilliant criminal defenders of the early 1900s. Darrow had defended the downtrodden, the unpopular, and the controversial in landmark cases, such as the Scopes "Monkey Trial" and the Scottsboro and Rosenberg trials.

Excerpted from *The Story of My Life*, by Clarence Darrow (New York: Charles Scribner's Sons, 1932). Copyright © 1932 by Charles Scribner's Sons. Reprinted by permission of the Estate of Clarence Darrow.

I deas have come and gone, but I have always been a champion of the individual as against the majority and the State. I advocate the fullest liberty of self-expression, and long before prohibition became the policy of the United States I had fought for the right of the individual to choose his own life. By that I mean, doing the things that he wants to do.

Of all the political leaders of the past, Thomas Jefferson made the strongest appeal to me. Personally, I never cared much for intoxicating liquor. I never drank to excess. I have occasionally taken wine or whiskey, but never regularly or in any way that could possibly be called a habit. So far as I personally was concerned, the use of liquor in any form would never have influenced or affected me, but in prohibition I saw a grievous and far-reaching menace to the right of the individual. I knew it was supported by all the forces that were hostile to human freedom. I foresaw that it meant a fanaticism and intolerance that would hesitate at nothing to force its wishes and ways of life upon the world. The line between what should be the rights of the individual and the power of the state has never been clearly drawn; in fact, no one can set down a hard and fast rule for settling the limitations with any certainty. Still, broadly speaking, humans are divided into two classes; one of these is always urging more laws and stricter rules for each and all; the other faction is ever doubtful and distrustful of authority, and does not believe in the wisdom of the mob. These thoughtful, inquiring ones fear the majority. They know how tyrannical and unscrupulous the majority has always been; they know the conceit of the ignorant, the intolerance of the bigot, and they instinctively fight for the rights of the individual against the crowd. In this contest I am, and always have been, with the individual battling for the right to express himself in his own life regardless of the mob. Essentially, the problem of prohibition, like many another, is a question of attitudes.

A History of Restrictive Measures

Long before the adoption of the Eighteenth Amendment and the Volstead Act, I did everything in my power with addresses in public and articles in periodicals to protest against the rising danger. For seventy-five or a hundred years most of the evangelical churches of America have been the meeting places for all sorts of restrictive measures. Beginning in the early colonies, especially in Massachusetts, capital punishment was inflicted for the practice of witchcraft. Under those statutes old women were hanged for an offense that never had any existence. The criminal code was one of the bloodiest that the world has ever known. If a child struck its parent it could be put to death, but the parent could strike the child with impunity. It was a crime to take a journey on Sunday. All sorts of work and play on the Sabbath were forbidden by the severest penalties. Many of these statutes are still in operation in the United States, and an organized society of fanatics send out their moronic literature and constantly appear before legislative bodies to urge penalties against any one who works or plays on the day they hold sacred, and to forbid all amusements and diversions of all sorts on Sunday except going to church. This is done on the theory that if there is no other place open on Sunday many people will feel compelled to go to church. Theatres were forbidden in New England not only on Sunday but on every day of the week. Even today the Methodist Association for Temperance Prohibition and Public Morals send out their literature denouncing the theatres.

This association, from its convenient vantage-ground, across the street from our National Capitol, keep men on guard to watch if perchance any one may smile on Sunday, or may have any real pleasure at any time. And then they browbeat and intimidate weak-kneed and weak-minded legislators to pass their absurd and outrageous laws. Their leaflets, that they send out by the million, urge all sorts of Sunday legislation. They condemn all dancing. They oppose all theatre-going. They propose legislation against the use of tobacco in every form, and card-playing is frowned upon. A world made over by this organization would banish all real enjoyment and entertainment from the earth.

Strong Liquor and Sparse Populations

The rural districts of America have always been over-whelmingly Protestant. Up to forty or fifty years ago the great majority of our people lived in villages and outlying sections. Such organizations as I have mentioned, together with the old-time temperance society, furnished the social life of the natives of a bygone period. The early emigrants from the country to the city carried with them the customs, habits, religion, and stern views of life that go with new communities. They were people who were converted by the old-time revivalists and were nourished upon the old prohibition speeches of men like Gough and Murphy, who were wont to go up and down the land inoculating their hearers with the religious and social bigotries that always prevail in the isolated passes and unfrequented stretches of a new nation. Literature, art, and learning were slow in reaching the waste and unready areas. The Protestant churches and lonely schoolhouses in the vast unsettled prairies were the centres of social exchange, and there was little incentive for original liberal ideas.

Cheap land, abundant natural resources, and hard work brought prosperity to the early settlers who drifted to America. This degree of wealth had been entirely unknown to their native life. Their good fortune gave them plenty to eat, and, when a peasant people first get plenty of food they eat too much; some of them also enjoyed getting something to drink, and it was not the beer and light wines they had known at home, but was the stronger liquors which are indigenous to sparse populations. They not only ate too much but they drank too much. Moderation in eating and drinking comes only with civilization and culture. No one paid any attention to over-eating, but over-drinking furnished a spectacular and colorful example to the propagandists. There were always more graves filled from over-eating than over-drinking, but the gluttons quietly groaned their lives away without exhibiting any hilarity or undue emotion in the process, and so were unmolested. On the contrary, the drunkards boisterously and riotously, and, to all appearances, with great glee reeled into their drunkards' graves.

Puritan Life Was Grim

Puritanism has always associated pleasure with sin. To the real Puritan, life is a grim, depressing duty; this earth is nothing but a preparatory school for entering heaven. And to be happy in heaven, one must be unhappy here. So the old revivalist and temperance reformer had no difficulty in holding up the drunkard as a horrible example: Just see how happy and carefree and unmeddlesome he was; always so satisfied with his lot in life and willing that every one else should do as he liked; naturally there was something wrong with such a method of living. The glutton dragged himself to the meeting and shouted "Amen!" in the right places, a friend to heartburn but not to hiccough. It was not difficult to teach the people that all the evil of this world came from *rum.*

The temperance societies, like The Good Templars, superintended the social gatherings. Their speeches were about *The Demon Rum.* Their songs were moving exhortations against rum and its dangers and downfalls; some of their favorite "recitations" were "Father, dear father, come home with me now," and "Lips that touch liquor shall never touch mine," which poetical classics, from generation to generation, would be followed with warnings about the first drop being the fatal one; after that there was small chance of saving the soul from everlasting damnation, so all the young men there must not wait another minute but come forward at once and sign the pledge and never go anywhere without the little white ribbon in the coat lapel to scare off the tempter.

A Dry Morality Play

Going to the theatre was forbidden, but the town halls and schools were permitted to present "Ten Nights in a Barroom," and this touching "mellow" drama furnished the old and young with all the histrionic art that was good for them. It was in vain that these primitive folk were told that few people of intelligence and culture ever lived who did not drink. It was in vain that the old classics mentioned the taking and enjoying of liquor as freely as the temperance preachers spoke of corned beef and cabbage and fried chicken with their savory flavors and odors.

Devouring all the food that one could hold was praiseworthy. But drinking liquor, even one mouthful, was damnable. No one talked temperance in eating, nor drinking—only total abstinence from *rum*. They read their Bibles, calmly forgetting the statement of Solomon, God's wisest man: "Give strong drink unto him that is ready to perish, and wine unto those that be of heavy heart. Let him drink and forget his poverty, and remember his misery no more."

They had church suppers on all the established religious holidays and anniversaries, and on as many local and special ones as they could invent and afford, these celebrations being chiefly competitions among the women to furnish the greatest possible amount of the richest, most palatable and irresistible, but wickedly indigestible and injurious, dishes, with each family donating a share of "refreshments" feeling insulted and hurt if any one declined to "taste it" and brag about it, and even take a second helping. Only when it became "impossible to swallow another mouthful," were they allowed to stop stuffing themselves with chicken, pork-and-beans, apple dumplings, cottage cheese, sausage and buckwheat cakes, corn muffins, noodles, cider and grapejuice, onions, waffles and honey, catsup, fried fish, sourkraut, headcheese, hot bread, jellies, soda biscuits, pigs' feet, sardines, coffee and doughnuts, crumpets, rich gravies, rice, and cream "that you could cut with a knife" and preserves and pickles and cucumber "delight" and homemade peppersauce and banana-fritters and horseradish and maple syrup, and root beer and cocoa and lemonade, and milk, and cold meats on the side, and salmon, and smoked raw ham and things like that for the first course; after that came mince pie, caramel custard, more coffee (of course), tarts, coconut kisses, seed cookies, floating island, combination salad with much mayonnaise, and no stint of whipped cream, and devil's food and angel's food and layer cakes, and ice cream and hot chocolate and suet-pudding and candy and raisins and nuts, until none of them could down another crumb that day. But each family carefully collected whatever was left over to take home and consume the next day before it could spoil, while the men and those who were not needed to help clear off the tables ranged themselves in the assembly hall and listened sanctimoniously to the sinfulness of even a sip of liquor and how such an act would forever disgrace the guilty one, and all his immediate family and even distant relatives. Every man should show his strength of character by totally abstaining from strong drink and come to church and gorge himself like a gentleman with the respectable people who are so much better off attending oyster festivals than rum debauches, because it is a crime to spend father's savings for too much *drink* instead of buying shoes with it for little Willie.

A Vow of Temperance

Then they unanimously offered a hearty vote of thanks for the good uplifting "remarks" and said that wine and real beer were the invention of Satan himself; once more they signed the pledge and solemnly vowed never to take a drink, and coaxed others to come forward and put their names down, too. Then, a soulful prayer asking that they might never weaken but stick to their pledge, and although they could hardly waddle they made their way home, where they managed to amble around long enough to concoct doses for indigestion and gas pains, mixing mustard plasters for the outside, while they couldn't understand why they should have gout, and were afraid the new doctor was not all that he should be because the pills he gave hadn't yet stopped the rheumatism that seemed to be coming on again. And with all the self-love of their kind they would have a last little chat about the excellent progress being made by the workers in saving people from too much liquor, and would absorb a few spoonfuls of sulphur-and-molasses because they thought they looked a little florid and their blood might be out of order. The next morning they would tell about not having slept well, and read advertisements to find out if possibly they might have liver complaint, on account of having a strange dizzy feeling every time they woke up in the night. They did not even know that a glass of rum would have helped digestion.

It was on this popular foundation that prohibitionists organized their forces and waged the campaign to destroy the liberties of American citizens. It was on this foundation that they foisted upon the United States a reign of terror, intimidation, violence, and bigotry unprecedented in the modern world.

Prohibition Is Contrary to Human Nature

Percy Andreae

> Percy Andreae was originally recruited by Ohio brewers to
> police unlawful abuses in saloons that made the liquor indus-
> try look negligent. He eventually became one of the most
> successful spokesmen against Prohibition. With considerable
> financial political backing from brewers, he was able to
> mount an effective campaign against the powerful Anti-
> Saloon League. Eventually Andreae took the campaign to a
> national level to fight the looming Eighteenth Amendment.
> But anti-Prohibition forces were too disorganized and weak-
> ened by internal conflict.
>
> In the following article, Andreae criticizes religious "drys"
> for their zealous attempts to take free choice out of the hands
> of the public. He believes their puritan efforts actually dis-
> guise a desire to impose religious ideology upon the nation.
> Such crusaders are blind to the economic and social damage
> Prohibition would entail. Andreae's stance is one that many
> anti-prohibitionists would use in debate. But Andreae takes it
> further and equates alcohol to other human vices, which have
> all existed in all men since the beginning of time. He believes
> alcohol is something that should not and simply cannot be
> controlled by law.

Excerpted from *The Prohibition Movement in Its Broader Bearings upon Our Social, Commercial, and Religious Liberties*, by Percy Andreae (Chicago: Felix Mendelsohn, 1915).

S omewhere in the Bible it is said: "If thy right hand offend thee, cut it off." I used to think the remedy somewhat radical. But today, being imbued with the wisdom of the prohibitionist, I have to acknowledge that, if the Bible in general, and that passage in it in particular, has a fault, it lies in its ultra-conservativeness. What? Merely cut off my own right hand if it offend me? What business have my neighbors to keep their right hands if I am not able to make mine behave itself? Off with the lot of them! Let there be no right hands; then I am certain that mine won't land me in trouble.

I have met many active prohibitionists, both in this and in other countries, all of them thoroughly in earnest. In some instances I have found that their allegiance to the cause of prohibition took its origin in the fact that some near relative or friend had succumbed to over-indulgence in liquor. In one or two cases the man himself had been a victim of this weakness, and had come to the conclusion, firstly that every one else was constituted as he was, and, therefore, liable to the same danger; and secondly, that unless every one were prevented from drinking, he would not be secure from the temptation to do so himself.

A Means to an End

This is one class of prohibitionists. The other, and by far the larger class, is made up of religious zealots, to whom prohibition is a word having at bottom a far wider application than that which is generally attributed to it. The liquor question, if there really is such a question per se, is merely put forth by them as a means to an end, an incidental factor in a fight which has for its object the supremacy of a certain form of religious faith. The belief of many of these people is that the Creator frowns upon enjoyment of any and every kind, and that he has merely endowed us with certain desires and capacities for pleasure in order to give us an opportunity to please Him by resisting them. They are, of course, perfectly entitled to this belief, though some of us may consider it eccentric and somewhat in the nature of a libel on the Almighty. But are they privileged to force that belief on all their fellow beings? That, in substance, is the question that is involved in the present-day prohibition movement.

For it is all nonsense to suppose that because, perhaps, one in a hundred or so of human beings is too weak to resist the temptation of over-indulging in drink—or of over-indulging in anything else, for the matter of that—therefore all mankind is going to forego the right to indulge in that enjoyment in moderation. The leaders of the so-called prohibition movement know as well as you and I do that you can no more prevent an individual from taking a drink if he be so inclined than you can prevent him from scratching himself if he itches. They object to the existence of the saloon, not, bear in mind, to that of the badly conducted saloon, but to that of the well-regulated, decent saloon, and wherever they succeed in destroying the latter, their object, which is the manifestation of their political power, is attained. That for every decent, well-ordered saloon they destroy, there springs up a dive, or speakeasy, or blind tiger, or whatever other name it may be known by, and the dispensing of drink continues as merrily as before, doesn't disturb them at all. They make the sale of liquor a crime, but steadily refuse to make its purchase and consumption an offense. Time and again the industries affected by this apparently senseless crusade have endeavored to have laws passed making dry territories really dry by providing for the punishment of the man who buys drink as well as the man who sells it. But every such attempt has been fiercely opposed by the prohibition leaders. And why? Because they know only too well that the first attempt to really prohibit drinking would put an end to their power forever. They know that 80 per cent of those who, partly by coercion, partly from sentiment, vote dry, are perfectly willing to restrict the right of the remaining 20 per cent to obtain drink, but that they are not willing to sacrifice that right for themselves.

Prohibition in Name Only

And so the farce called prohibition goes on, and will continue to go on as long as it brings grist to the mill of the managers who are producing it. But the farce conceals something far more serious than that which is apparent to the public on the face of it. Prohibition is merely the title of the movement. Its real purpose is of a religious, sectarian character, and this applies not only to the movement in America, but to the same movement in England, a fact which, strangely enough, has rarely, if at all, been recognized by those who have dealt with the question in the public press.

If there is any one who doubts the truth of this statement, let me put this to him: How many Roman Catholics are prohibitionists? How many Jews, the most temperate race on earth, are to be found in the ranks of prohibition? Or Lutherans? Or German Protestants generally? What is the proportion of Episcopalians to that of Methodists, Baptists and Presbyterians, and the like, in the active prohibition army? The answer to these questions will, I venture to say, prove conclusively the assertion that the fight for prohibition is synonymous with the fight of a certain religious sect, or group of religious sects, for the supremacy of its ideas. In England it is the Nonconformists, which is in that country the generic name for the same sects, who are fighting the fight, and the suppression of liquor there is no more the ultimate end they have in view than it is here in America. It is the fads and restrictions that are part and parcel of their lugubrious notion of God-worship which they eventually hope to impose upon the rest of humanity; a Sunday without a smile, no games, no recreation, no pleasures, no music, card-playing tabooed, dancing anathematized, the beauties of art decried as impure—in short, this world reduced to a barren, forbidding wilderness in which we, its inhabitants, are to pass our time contemplating the joys of the next. Rather problematical joys, by the way, if we are to suppose we shall worship God in the next world in the same somber way as we are called upon by these worthies to do in this.

To my mind, and that of many others, the hearty, happy laugh of a human being on a sunny Sunday is music sweeter to the ears of that being's Creator than all the groaning and moanings, and *misericordias* [songs of mercy] that rise to heaven from the lips of those who would deprive us altogether of the faculty and the privilege of mirth. That some overdo hilarity and become coarse and offensive, goes without saying. There are people without the sense of proportion or propriety in all matters. Yet none of us think of abolishing pleasures because a few do not know how to enjoy them in moderation and with decency, and become an offense to their neighbors.

The drink evil has existed from time immemorial, just as sexual excess has, and all other vices to which mankind is and always will be more or less prone, though less in proportion as education progresses and the benefits of civilization increased. Sexual excess, curiously enough, has never interested our hyper-religious friends, the prohibitionists, in anything like the degree that the vice of excessive drinking does. Perhaps this is because the best of us have our pet aversions and our pet weaknesses. Yet this particular vice has produced more evil results to the human race than all other vices combined, and, in spite of it, mankind, thanks not to prohibitive laws and restrictive legislation, but to the forward strides of knowledge and to patient and intelligent education, is today ten times sounder in body and healthier in mind than it ever was in the world's history.

Now, if the habit of drinking to excess were a growing one, as our prohibitionist friends claim that it is, we should today, instead of discussing this question with more or less intelligence, not be here at all to argue it; for the evil, such as it is, has existed for so many ages that, if it were as general and as contagious as is claimed, and its results as far-reaching as they are painted, the human race would have been destroyed by it long ago. Of course, the contrary is the case. The world has progressed in this as in all other respects. Compare, for instance, the drinking today with the drinking of a thousand years ago, nay, of only a hundred odd years ago, when a man, if he wanted to ape his so-called betters, did so by contriving to be carried to bed every night "drunk as a lord." Has that condition of affairs been altered by legislative measures restricting the right of the individual to control himself? No. It has been altered by that far greater power, the moral force of education and the good example which teaches mankind the very thing that prohibition would take from it: the virtue of self-control and moderation in all things.

Prohibition Goes Against Human Nature

And here we come to the vital distinction between the advocacy of temperance and the advocacy of prohibition. Temperance and self-control are convertible terms. Prohibition, or that which it implies, is the direct negation of the term self-control. In order to save the small percentage of men who are too weak to resist their animal desires, it aims to put chains on every man, the weak and the strong alike. And if this is proper in one respect, why not in all respects? Yet, what would one think of a proposition to keep all men locked up because a certain number have a propensity to steal? Theoretically, perhaps, all crime or vice could be stopped by chaining us all up as we chain up a wild animal, and only allowing us to take exercise under proper supervision and control. But while such a measure would check crime, it would not eliminate the criminal. It is true, some people are only kept from vice and crime by the fear of punishment. Is not, indeed, the basis of some men's religiousness nothing else but the fear of Divine punishment? The doctrines of certain religious denominations not entirely unknown in the prohibition camp make self-respect, which is the foundation of self-control and of all morality, a sin. They decry rather than advocate it. They love to call themselves miserable, helpless sinners, cringing before the flaming sword, and it is the flaming sword, not the exercise of their own enlightened will, that keeps them within decent bounds. Yet has this fear of eternal punishment contributed one iota toward the intrinsic betterment of the human being? If it had, would so many of our Christian creeds have discarded it, admitting that it is the precepts of religion, not its dark and dire threats, that make men truly better and stronger within themselves to resist that which our self-respect teaches us is bad and harmful? The growth of self-respect in man, with its outward manifestation, self-control, is the growth of civilization. If we are to be allowed to exercise it no longer, it must die in us from want of nutrition, and men must become savages once more, fretting now at their chains, which they will break as inevitably as the sun will rise tomorrow and herald a new day.

Prohibitionists Underestimate Mankind

I consider the danger which threatens civilized society from the growing power of a sect whose views on prohibition are merely an exemplification of their general low estimate of man's ability to rise to higher things—by his own volition to be of infinitely greater consequence than the danger that, in putting their narrow theories to the test, a few billions of invested property will be destroyed, a number of great wealth-producing industries wiped out, the rate of individual taxation largely increased, and a million or so of struggling wage earners doomed to face starvation. These latter considerations, of course, must appeal to every thinking man but what are they compared with the greater questions involved? Already the government of our State, and indeed of a good many other States, has passed practically into the hands of a few preacher-politicians of a certain creed. With the machine they have built up, by appealing to the emotional weaknesses of the more or less unintelligent masses, they have lifted themselves on to a pedestal of power that has enabled them to dictate legislation or defeat it at their will, to usurp the functions of the governing head of the State and actually induce him to delegate to them the appointive powers vested in him by the Constitution. When a Governor elected by the popular vote admits, as was recently the case, that he can not appoint a man to one of the most important offices of the State without the indorsement of the irresponsible leader of a certain semi-religious movement, and when he submits to this same personage for correction and amendment his recommendation to the legislative body, there can scarcely be any doubt left in any reasonable mind as to the extent of the power wielded by this leader, or as to the uses he and those behind him intend putting it to.

The Most Dangerous Form of Government

And what does it all mean? It means that government by emotion is to be substituted for government by reason, and government by emotion, of which history affords many examples, is, according to the testimony of all ages, the most dangerous and pernicious of all forms of government. It has already crept into the legislative assemblies of most of the States of the Union, and is being craftily fostered by those who know how easily it can be made available for their purposes—purposes to the furtherance of which cool reason would never lend itself. Prohibition is but one of its fruits, and the hand that is plucking this fruit is the same hand of intolerance that drove forth certain of our forefathers from the land of their birth to seek the sheltering freedom of these shores.

What a strange reversal of conditions! The intolerants of a few hundred years ago are the upholders of liberty today, while those they once persecuted, having multiplied by grace of the very liberty that has so long sheltered them here, are now planning to impose the tyranny of their narrow creed upon the descendants of their persecutors of yore.

Let the greater public, which is, after all, the arbiter of the country's destinies, pause and ponder these things before they are allowed to progress too far. Prohibition, though it must cause, and is already causing, incalculable damage, may never succeed in this country; but that which is behind it, as the catapults and the cannon were behind the battering rams in the battles of olden days, is certain to succeed unless timely measures of prevention are resorted to; and if it does succeed, we shall witness the enthronement of a monarch in this land of liberty compared with whose autocracy the autocracy of the Russian Czar is a mere trifle.

The name of this monarch is Religious Intolerance.

Prohibition Is Unenforceable

Fiorello H. La Guardia

Before the passage of the Eighteenth Amendment, prominent
New York politician Fiorello H. La Guardia theorized that
Prohibition would be impossible to enforce. He warned fellow congressman Andrew Volstead (author of the enforcement legislation bearing his name) that failure to enforce
Prohibition would only breed contempt for the law. Unfortunately, all of La Guardia's predictions came true. By 1926
violations of the Volstead Act by career criminals as well as
ordinary citizens were too numerous to count. Government
corruption had also become widespread. The Prohibition laws
were even being broken within the hallowed halls of Congress by supposedly "dry" politicians. The following is a
statement La Guardia made in 1926 before a Senate committee about Prohibition policy failure. In it, La Guardia insists
that present laws cannot be enforced and that modifications
will have to be made in order for Prohibition to succeed.

It is impossible to tell whether prohibition is a good thing
or a bad thing. It has never been enforced in this country.

There may not be as much liquor in quantity consumed
to-day as there was before prohibition, but there is just as
much alcohol.

At least 1,000,000 quarts of liquor are consumed each
day in the United States. In my opinion such an enormous
traffic in liquor could not be carried on without the knowl-

Excerpted from *Hearings Before the Subcommittee of the Committee on the Judiciary,
United States Senate, Sixty-Ninth Congress*, vol. 1, by the United States Senate (Washington, DC: Government Printing Office, 1926).

edge, if not the connivance of the officials entrusted with the enforcement of the law.

I am for temperance, that is why I am for modification.

I believe that the percentage of whisky drinkers in the United States now is greater than in any other country of the world. Prohibition is responsible for that.

I am ready to concede the absolute good faith and sincerity of the greater number of dry leaders in this country. I do not believe they are hypocrites and insincere any more than I believe that every advocate for modification of the law is a rum hound and a drunkard.

I consider the W.C.T.U. [Woman's Christian Temperance Union] one of the greatest organizations that has ever existed in this country. Prior to prohibition they did more constructive work for temperance in one day than the prohibition laws have done in five years. I am certain that once the splendid women composing the W.C.T.U. know and understand real conditions and what prohibition is doing, they will change their present views.

There are a few rascals and scoundrels among the drys just as there are among the wets.

Everybody Profits Except the Government

At least $1,000,000,000 a year is lost to the National Government and the several States and counties in excise taxes. The liquor traffic is going on just the same. This amount goes into the pockets of bootleggers and in the pockets of the public officials in the shape of graft.

In 1919 the Federal Government received in taxes on spirits and fermented liquors a total of $483,050,854.47.

In the fiscal year 1925 the Federal Government received on beverage alcohol spirits $2,725,933.88.

A comparison of the amount of spirits used in these two years will be interesting. I venture to state that there is slight variance in the quantity of alcohol which was actually consumed in the two years cited.

I will concede that the saloon was odious but now we have delicatessen stores, pool rooms, drug stores, millinery shops, private parlors, and 57 other varieties of speak-easies selling liquor and flourishing.

I have heard of $2,000 a year prohibition agents who run their own cars with liveried chauffeurs.

It is common talk in my part of the country that from $7.50 to $12 a case is paid in graft from the time the liquor leaves the 12-mile limit[1] until it reaches the ultimate consumer. There seems to be a varying market price for this service created by the degree of vigilance or the degree of greed of the public officials in charge.

It is my calculation that at least a million dollars a day is paid in graft and corruption to Federal, State, and local officers. Such a condition is not only intolerable, but it is demoralizing and dangerous to organized government.

It would seem that even the Government engages in a sideline of bootlegging. The consumption of denatured alcohol since prohibition has increased over 200 per cent. Making a generous allowance for the use of denatured alcohol for legitimate industrial purposes, several million gallons of denatured poison alcohol, sold under Government permits, is cooked, colored, flavored, and sold as liquor all over the country.

If the Government tomorrow would stop issuing permits for denatured alcohol under the high numbered formulas, you would see the greatest collection of politicians from all over the country that had ever gathered before in Washington protesting to the Bureau of Internal Revenue and demanding the reissuance of those permits. As long as the Government issues permits to withdraw denatured or industrial alcohol, so long will the market be flooded with poison hootch.

I know of no other test of prohibition of greater importance to the dry advocates than the control and curbing of the traffic in denatured alcohol. Why do not the drys use their influence in stopping the Government issuing permits

---

1. U.S. waters formerly extended out to 3 miles, but this was changed to make it more difficult for rumrunners.

for millions and millions of gallons of denatured alcohol? I will join with any movement of the drys to stop this vicious traffic. It is entirely up to the Government.

The Government even goes to the trouble to facilitate the financing end of the bootlegging industry. In 1925, $268,950,000 more of $10,000 bills, were issued than in 1920 and $25,000,000 more of $5,000 bills were issued. What honest business man deals in $10,000 bills? Surely these bills were not used to pay the salaries of ministers. The bootlegging industry has created a demand for bills of large denominations, and the Treasury Department accommodates them.

Everybody Is an Accomplice

The drys seemingly are afraid of the truth. Why not take inventory and ascertain the true conditions. Let us not leave it to the charge of an antiprohibition organization, or to any other private association, let us have an official survey and let the American people know what is going on. A complete and honest and impartial survey would reveal incredible conditions, corruption, crime, and an organized system of illicit traffic such as the world has never seen.

The drys are in complete control of the House of Representatives. The drys in the House outnumber the wets three to one. Yet it is impossible to get the approval of the House for a survey. I do not know conditions in the Senate, therefore simply refer to the House.

As long as the drys are preventing a thorough investigation and survey of the conditions in this country on alcoholic liquor traffic, they are unwittingly, perhaps, but actually aiding and abetting the bootlegging industry.

The bootlegging fraternity is getting more powerful each day. Once a public official wavers he is entirely in their clutches and at their mercy. The bootleggers have no better friends than the extreme drys, who insist upon keeping their eyes closed and refuse to see the truth and actual conditions.

The Prohibition Enforcement Unit has entirely broken down. It is discredited, it has become a joke. Liquor is sold in every large city. The amount consumed, as I have stated before, is so enormous that it must be imported, manufactured, and transported to such an extent that would be impossible if enforcement officials were not either corrupt or

Financial Reasons

The "wet" propagandists focused on several economic points in their arguments, some of which included the destruction of the liquor industry and the loss of jobs, crime, and the loss of liquor tax income by the government. But historian Andrew Sinclair writes the wealthy "wets" also had an economic motive.

Throughout the twenties, the level of federal income had averaged three billion dollars a year, of which more than two-thirds came from taxes on incomes and corporations. The wealthy in America were paying three-quarters of a billion dollars a year on their private incomes. They were looking for some way to shed the load. Repeal of national prohibition seemed to be that way.

Indeed, if the tax situation of the wealthy is considered, national prohibition seems to have been an inefficient means of redistributing the wealth of America. The workingmen of America drank half their usual amount of liquor and saved one billion dollars a year. The middle classes drank the same amount of liquor and lost one billion dollars a year. The federal government lost something over half a billion dollars a year on liquor taxes, which it made up on income taxes from the rich and the corporations. Moreover, between one and two billion dollars were transferred from wealthy brewers and distillers to the *nouveaux riches* among the criminal classes, and from them to the underpaid judges and attorneys and policemen of the United States. Altogether, prohibition was a sort of irresponsible Robin Hood, stealing from the rich and giving to the poor. Only, unlike Robin Hood, prohibition was not thanked by the poor for its pains.

Andrew Sinclair, *Prohibition: The Era of Excess.* New York: Atlantic Monthly Press, 1962.

incompetent. Only a few days ago I charged on the floor of the House that 350 cases of liquor of a seizure of 1,500 cases made by Federal officials and stored in the Federal building at Indianapolis, Ind., had been removed. The Department of Justice, under date of April 9, 1926, confirmed my charge. The Attorney General admits that since this liquor was in the possession of the Federal authorities in the Federal building at Indianapolis, 330 cases are missing. If bootleggers can enter Federal buildings to get liquor the rest can be easily imagined.

There is a great deal of "monkey business" going on in the transfers of liquor from one distillery to another. An investigation along these lines would reveal astonishing and startling facts.

I have been in public office for a great many years. I have had the opportunity to observe first the making of the present prohibition laws as a Member of Congress, and later as president of the board of aldermen of the largest city in this country its attempted enforcement. In order to enforce prohibition in New York City I estimated at the time would require a police force of 250,000 men and a force of 200,000 men to police the police.

Testing the Law

From my observation and from my direct contact as a municipal official I believe that the law is impossible of enforcement. If the drys want another chance and a test, I do not see why they should not be given every opportunity to test this law. I don't mean legally but practicably. This is the month of April. The President of the United States and his administration are pledged to strict enforcement. As I have said before, the drys are in the majority in the House. Why not have the President remove the present director and all the officials in the Prohibition Unit and appoint any prominent person of the Anti-Saloon League, for instance, Mr. Wayne Wheeler himself. Appoint as regional directors and in every place of command men and women indorsed and approved by the extreme dry advocates. Let Congress give them all they ask for. Let them do anything they desire to enforce this law. We will come back to the short session in December. Let them come in in January or February and make a report. I predict that they would have to admit that the prohibition law can not be enforced and must be modified. Then we can get together and do it.

Personally I believe that to modify the enforcement laws it will be necessary to amend the Constitution. That is simply my personal opinion.

What modification of the law, I believe, would mean:

1. It would create temperance.

2. It would stop corruption and graft of public officials, restore confidence in the Government and respect for the law.

3. It would consume hundreds of millions of bushels of grain now a surplus on the market, a burden to the country, and a dead loss to the farmers.

4. It would bring in hundreds of millions of dollars in excise taxes now entirely lost to communities, counties, States, and Government.

5. It would stop the growing habit of whisky drinking and poison guzzling.

6. It would put strong liquor under absolute control.

7. It would stop making America the laughingstock of the world.

8. It would decrease crime.

9. It would compel many politicians to do an honest day's work for a living.

10. It would permit the people to think about more important economic problems and would stop loss of time in endless discussions of the booze question.

11. It would permit every community to decide for itself whether it wanted to be dry or moist.

Chapter 3

The Cops and the Criminals

Chapter Preface

In no other time in history was the line blurred between lawmen and criminals as it was during Prohibition. It was often difficult to tell one from the other since their relationship became symbiotic. Gangsters helped political candidates, such as Mayor William Hale Thompson of Chicago, get elected to office. And in return, corrupt politicians issued permits to bootleggers or turned a blind eye to their operations.

The problem worsened after the onset of the Great Depression in 1929. Towering unemployment and the public's frustration with government contributed to the delinquency of ordinary citizens. Many of these citizens had never broken the law before and clogged up the legal system after being caught. Ironically, they were sometimes acquitted by sympathetic juries who also believed the law to be unjust.

On the streets of major cities across the country, gangland murders were on the rise, yet so were shooting deaths by incompetent Prohibition agents. It is estimated that over one thousand people were killed by Prohibition agents and the Coast Guard during the Prohibition era. Public backlash was fierce, and many local law enforcement agencies retreated from the bad publicity and left Prohibition enforcement up to federal authorities. Overall, Prohibition became a difficult and unpopular law to enforce.

In 1930, President Hoover appointed a special commission to study Prohibition and its enforcement problems. The panel was led by former attorney general George W. Wickersham. Although the Wickersham Commission stated it was opposed to repeal, many of the members of the group stated that they considered Prohibition to be unenforceable. This contradictory conclusion just angered opponents and supporters of Prohibition and highlighted the fact that there were no easy solutions in implementing the new law.

Prohibition Agent No. 1

Izzy Einstein

> Prohibition agents were not popular people during the twenties.
> They enforced a law that many Americans did not agree with.
> They were further stigmatized because many agents were
> known to accept bribes from bootleggers, which made the
> entire bureau seem corrupt. Izzy Einstein was an exception. His
> unorthodox methods netted 4,932 arrests. Einstein had once
> been a salesman and used his people skills to put suspicious
> bartenders at ease. He also used disguises and clever ruses, as
> illustrated in this excerpt from Einstein's autobiography.
>
> Despite his lack of police experience, Einstein eclipsed his
> fellow Prohibition agents. It was, however, that overwhelming
> success that would eventually get Einstein fired. The press
> loved Einstein and frequently published articles about him, but
> this publicity drew unwanted attention. His supervisors
> thought the publicity made a mockery of justice.

Salt air is peculiar. Why does this damp air make seaside
throats dry (especially if they've just come from the city)
and seaside hotels wet?

Frankly I couldn't figure it.

Not being able to and yet unwilling to confess myself permanently buffaloed, I decided to see what might be learned
by sniffing the atmosphere in the vicinity of a certain hotel
at Rockaway, Long Island.

This hotel, patronized less for its sleeping facilities than for its standing-up ones at the bar, was doing so well that the proprietor thought he needed more scope; he was having an addition built on. It was a case of getting ready to flout the law in a bigger way—for no agent had been able to get him and he felt confident that none could.

But I felt different when I saw carpenters on the job there. It was my cue. After one preliminary look from a safe distance, I paid a business visit, and this time I was in overalls with a carpenter's rule sticking out of my upper pocket and a saw in my hand. Walked in, asked for the proprietor, and struck him for a job.

"Guess we've got all the men we need right now," he said. "But maybe later there might be a chance, if you stick around."

He didn't have to urge me. And while I was sticking around, I took the opportunity of looking around.

"Say, that's quite a bar you've got there," I remarked to him. "Must be all of sixty feet."

"No, not that long. Less than fifty."

"It's sixty feet or I'm no carpenter," I told him. "And what's more I'll bet you on it."

He said I was crazy, but I stuck to my sixty feet. Offered to pay for a round of drinks for every one in the house if I was wrong.

We measured—with five or six volunteer judges looking on—and I was wrong. The bet was poured and I paid. Then I slipped across the street and bought liquor in the place opposite—and came back and arrested the man I bet with.

He was very upset. Said he was a family man with daughters, one of them a school-teacher. For him to be arrested as a bootlegger would put a cruel blemish on them.

I consoled him by mentioning that his rival across the street was in the same boat. This news seemed to soothe him wonderfully and I collected the two of them.

The Wet Shore

Coney Island was a simpler proposition. People there were so busy pulling in the suckers, they overlooked the possibility that they might get pulled in themselves. At many a place all I had to do was to appear in the guise of a shivering bather asking, "Any chance for a real drink to warm a fellow up?"

Some places there you didn't even need a bathing suit to get in on the wet. You just mentioned the water and got something else. For instance, at a drug store on Brighton Beach Avenue (it was near where you come out of the subway) I dropped in with a couple of other agents and we asked for a soft rubber ball to play with in swimming. Just then all the lights went out and candles were placed on the refreshment tables where we noticed people were sitting longer than is usual for soda drinkers. So we joined those resting in the dimly lighted store and suggested thirstily,

"How about another kind of ball—one with some Scotch in it?"

Prohibition agents Izzy Einstein (right) and Moe Smith share a toast at a New York bar. Einstein often used clever ruses to put suspicious bartenders at ease.

This visit was so successful we decided to celebrate by having a little something to eat at a big restaurant on Surf Avenue. But we didn't "eat" all the "food" listed on our check, which included such items as "1 lobster," and "1 crab"— meaning a bottle of wine and a Manhattan cocktail. To cure them of the error of their ways we pinched the place.

Law-violating in a more expensive, high-class style was

to be found at places further out. Long Beach, for example. And to the limousine trade Long Beach meant Nassau Hotel. It was a hotel where just anybody who happened to be listed in Dun and Bradstreet was sure of plentiful service—especially if he remembered to bring the contents of his safe deposit box along. Paupers and Prohibition agents weren't wanted.

Bound that I wouldn't be discriminated against, I rolled up to the door one evening about six o'clock with a "party of friends," including a couple of swell blondes. I myself was in white flannels, white shoes, and Panama hat, and I twiddled a cane. We barged into the dining room as if we owned it, and we had a right to feel that way after what I paid the head waiter for a table by the window.

Otherwise, I was so busy discussing real estate—how much an option on the Singer Building would cost me—I hardly had time to order the drinks.

"Anything else?" the waiter asked at the conclusion of our little meal, preparing to draw up the big check. I paid him first and then I told him; and then the pinch was so quiet that the hundred or so other people there didn't know anything about it except that the place had suddenly dried up.

Mixing with the Smart Set

Switching, for a change, to the more exclusive North Shore, I did an act at Smallwood's roadhouse in Glen Cove, near where Mr. J.P. Morgan [American financier and industrialist] and some of his friends have their summer cottages. Here I drove up in a Packard with another agent as my liveried chauffeur; I being a big mining man from the West, in a bright silk shirt and yellow spats, come to see what the Long Island Smart Set could do in the way of shaking an ankle. It was 1 A.M. when I arrived and there were at least two hundred of them busy at it, stopping for refreshments in between—until I ended all that by inviting the head waiter and my waiter to have a little ride into town to the Federal Building.

Woodmansten Inn, Joe Pani's famous roadhouse on Pelham Parkway, was another pippin ready to be pinched—if you could get in there without being spotted. Well, I trotted out my Broadway glad rags [dress clothes] and staged the same old limousine approach that had worked elsewhere. And they fell, the same as any new audience does for the magician's pet trick that he's been using these twenty years. Anyhow, I had no trouble getting tabled among the high-flyers, nor the least difficulty about buying drinks at $1.25 per. The hardship came afterwards, when I had sprung my news: I had to sit up the rest of the night guarding all the stuff I confiscated, as our trucks couldn't get out there till morning. That job, with no orchestra or floor show to help me in my knock-down-and-drag-out battle with sleep, was *some* assignment for a "gay sport" in a dress suit to hand himself. I can't say, though, that my fatigue was much grieved over by the management. It was what I was guarding that they were upset about. And what was ahead of them.

Wayside Filling Station

Among other out-of-town resorts I remember the name Roth House. And with good reason. This combination inn and cabaret, located at 180 Main Street, New Rochelle, the town that was "Forty-five Minutes from Broadway" according to George M. Cohan [American actor, songwriter, and playwright] some years ago, but is only half an hour now, had facilities such as few hotels were able to offer or even think up. That is to say, it fronted upon the Boston Post Road for the convenience of motorists, and (still thinking of them) had at its back a small inlet of Long Island Sound, which made possible the landing of liquor "right off the boat." Hence you might call it a wayside filling station that could never be emptied because of its unlimited supply.

Anxious to study the wonders of this unique establishment, I arrived there, bag and baggage, in the guise of a wealthy real estate man. Took the best suite they had, saying I didn't know just how long I'd stay; it depended on a deal I was putting through. Meanwhile my interest in real estate prompted me to cast a professional eye around the hotel itself. I noticed that the bar was quite a good piece of architecture, well varnished, well kept up, and apparently quite ably operated by a negro bartender.

When I let this colored gentleman know whom he had sold liquor to, he fainted. So I knew, from other cases where such a thing had happened, that there must be a good-sized hoard on the premises. And, sure enough, I found, down in the basement, a secret room containing $25,000 worth.

Then it was the proprietor who was taken weak.

Maybe his ship had just come in and this was the cargo. If so, the next time it arrived the dear old place wouldn't be quite the same.

I, myself, dabbled in a little boat-work out at Oyster Bay Harbor. Not that I ever joined the rum-chaser fleet; no, this was just something special, due to my happening to pick up a bit of information about a yacht that was due to sneak in there at midnight. When it appeared—you could see it picking a place to anchor, out just beyond the reflection of Lloyd's Neck Light—I was right in my element: terra firma. And I was watching. I watched a small yawl [two-masted sailboat] put ashore with a load, and I was ready on the shore when it came in, with a little speech in the name of the government, case of "yawl received and contents noted." Except that instead of one case there were one hundred and ten of them. And a bootlegger's motor truck waiting handy for me to confiscate it and commandeer it at the same time, with plenty of prisoners to do the heavy work.

So I felt that my outing in the salt air had been beneficial.

Incidentally we copped the yacht, which was called the *Jessie B.* And I'd always wanted a yacht.

The Danger of Unfit Prohibition Agents

Mabel Walker Willebrandt

Prohibition is considered one of the most lawless periods in modern American history. Besides the widespread violations of the law by gangsters as well as ordinary citizens, Prohibition agents themselves regularly committed crimes. There were many reported incidents of innocent people being killed and property being regularly seized and destroyed. There was even an incident in which a large Canadian ship was illegally sunk when it was suspected of rum-running.

Mabel Walker Willebrandt was the assistant attorney general of the United States in charge of Prohibition cases for eight difficult years. After Herbert Hoover was elected president in 1929, Willebrandt resigned her post. She published a series of articles about Prohibition in the *New York Times,* including the following article about the rash of deaths at the hands of Prohibition agents. Though she does not justify the deaths, she realizes their inevitability. Willebrandt supported Prohibition. But she fully understood the difficulties in enforcing the law. In her article she writes about unqualified agents who just made the problem worse.

"Is it necessary for prohibition agents to kill 135 persons in the course of less than 10 years in order to enforce prohibition?" is one of the questions I have been asked many times.

I might make an evasive answer to this question by asking another:

"Does not the killing of fifty-five agents of the prohibition unit in the same period, the killing of six Federal Coast Guard officers and the crippling of six others for life, and the killing of three narcotic enforcement officers and nine customs agents indicate the necessity for the use of arms and force by officers of the government to deal with a vast class of desperados engaged in criminal violations of the nation's laws?"

I have no desire, however, to evade the issue.

I not only believe, I know, that the violence which has accompanied enforcement or attempted enforcement of the prohibition law has done more than anything else, probably, to instill in the public mind the question and the doubt: "Can prohibition ever be enforced, and if so, is it worth the price in human life and the violation of personal and property rights?"

I also know, however, that all the facts about the violence that has attended enforcement of the prohibition law have not been adequately and properly submitted to the great body of the American people, who are the jury which in the end will return a verdict on the enforceability of the Eighteenth Amendment.

Looking at Both Sides

If I thought that enforcement of the prohibition law would necessarily entail continued killing and other acts of violence, and the outrage of private rights of persons and property, I would unqualifiedly demand the repeal of the Eighteenth Amendment and the laws enacted thereunder.

I condemn as atrocious, wholly unwarranted and entirely unnecessary some of the killing by the prohibition agents. But I know that there are equally shocking cases of gangsters' attacks on agents, which, if as widely known, will influence fair-minded people not to be too hasty in lavishing sympathy on violators of the law who get wounded in the course of arrest.

As a sample of how the bootlegger deals with citizens who stand in his way, this touching letter to me stands as mute evidence:

Dear Madam:

I understand that my husband wrote to you some time ago about prohibition law, and the agents you sent here told those, the wholesalers, about him writing to you, so the wholesalers went to the priest on the fourth of April. This priest called on my husband and warned him that the wholesalers would make a lot of trouble. Just four days after that they murdered my husband, Eugene Costa, and left me with five little children. My husband fought for his country during the World's War. And it took a foreigner to murder my husband over beer and whiskey. If you sent some one in I will explain it better. If you think it would be better for me to come there, please tell me when and how. For I am broken hearted.

Kindly pay special attention,

Mrs. Eugene Costa.

The Case of Tom Morris

Take the case of Tom Morris, deceased. His family now know that in enforcing the prohibition law agents of the government are not dealing with mere "good-hearted boys" who meet a public demand for liquor.

He, with another officer, stopped a car which was crossing the border loaded with liquor. After making the arrest and putting handcuffs on one of the men who had been in the car, the other said: "Wait a minute till I light a cigarette." The officer "waited a minute," but instead of lighting a cigarette the rum-runner pulled a gun and shot Morris, who died almost instantly. The defendant then ran and the surviving officer shot at him but missed. Subsequently captured and convicted, he was given only a prison term of from two to twenty years.

These bootleggers were the type ordinarily engaged in running liquor between Texas towns. Nothing in their appearance gave the agents warning. They were no better and no worse than thousands of other bootleggers who are operating daily in all parts of the country. And let it be remembered that the man who committed this act of violence was himself in no great danger from the law prior to the shooting of the customs officer. He was subject to a penalty at most of only six months and a few hundred dollars' fine after conviction. Nevertheless, in an attempt to avoid facing that charge he shot down and killed an officer of the law.

Indicted for Self-Defense

The case cited is not at all unusual. On Sept. 26, 1928, a prohibition agent named King stopped an automobile crossing a bridge at Jacksonville, Fla., and arrested a well-known bootlegger who was in charge of the load of liquor. When the agent stepped on the running board of the car the bootlegger pulled a gun and shot the agent, who fell into the road. Wounded as he was, King nevertheless managed to draw his own gun, and as the bootlegger started to drive away a running battle occurred in which Agent King killed the bootlegger. A disinterested workman on the bridge told the facts.

While the agent lay at the point of death in a hospital the State authorities, as the result of sensational and unwarranted press reports which inflamed the public mind and following threats of death from the deceased's associates, endeavored to obtain an indictment for murder against an officer who had risked his life in the performance of his legal duty and who had shot after being thrown in the road, wounded, and only in self-defense.

I might cite dozens of other similar cases, but I will call attention to only one more. It is the case of the *United States of America vs. James H. Alderman*, charged with and convicted of murder and sentenced to death. The conviction has been upheld by the United States Circuit Court of Appeals for the Fifth Circuit, and the Supreme Court of the United States has refused to review the case. The facts are these:

A Murder at Sea

On Aug. 7, 1927, a United States Coast Guard patrol boat, on duty off the coast of Florida, stopped a small boat coming from the direction of Bimini in the British West Indies and headed toward the Florida coast. On boarding the boat the Coast Guard commander, Sidney C. Sanderlin, found one James H. Alderman in charge, with Robert K. Weech aboard, together with twenty sacks of liquor. Of the Coast Guard boat crew, only Sanderlin was armed. He searched Alderman for weapons and found none.

While the Coast Guard crew was transferring the liquor from the small boat to the Coast Guard boat, Sanderlin started toward the pilot house of the patrol boat where his wireless was located, and Alderman followed him. A moment later the Coast Guard crew heard shots and saw Alderman, an automatic in his hand, take a step or two from the pilot house door and shoot at a member of the crew named Lamby. The shot struck Lamby and he fell into the engine room. No one saw Alderman shoot Sanderlin; but afterward Sanderlin was found dead on the floor of the pilot house, killed by a bullet which entered the right side of his back, passing through the heart and coming out of the left breast. Lamby died four days later in a Florida hospital.

Alderman, the bootleg runner, then lined up the remainder of the Coast Guard crew and, menacing them with his revolver, said that he was going to "get" the rest of them. He then directed his own companion, Weech, to get the liquor back aboard their boat, tear out the gas pipe of the patrol boat and set it afire. Alderman told the patrol crew that he was going to throw them overboard one at a time and shoot them, and that they might as well say their prayers, because they were all going to hell and they would need them.

Meanwhile, he had secured two more revolvers from the pilot house and had given one to his associate, Weech, so that the prisoners were covered by three guns. A few minutes later Alderman glanced down the hatch to see what Weech was doing with regard to the motor which he had ordered Weech to start. Taking advantage of his momentary inattention, the surviving members of the Coast Guard crew rushed toward Alderman and he began shooting. He succeeded in shooting one of them through the shoulder and head and in killing another. However, the others overcame him and later captured his associate, Weech.

Bootleggers Mostly "Killers"

I have outlined the facts in this case to show what vicious criminals are in the bootleg business, and the risk of his life an agent runs.

It is the officer's duty to make arrests. The law gives the arrested man every presumption of innocence and much legal protection. But he must go peaceably with the arresting officer to the nearest magistrate for hearing. Resisting an officer is a serious offense. It has been such ever since governments were established. It has been the duty of all sworn officers of the law to bring in their prisoners "dead or alive." That has always, since the days of Blackstone [Sir William Blackstone (1723–1780), English jurist and professor whose writings influenced common law in early America], been regarded as vital to the protection of society and the preservation of the State.

In dozens of cases—hundreds in fact—arrested bootleggers are resisting, with force and with guns, officers of the law who have the legal right and the duty to make the arrest and are discharging that duty lawfully. In no other class of cases has there been so much resistance to officers.

Every day, in some part of the United States, men are arrested by State and Federal officers for burglary, robbery, arson, mail robbery and other crimes for which the penalties are much more severe than those imposed for bootlegging. Yet there is no such resistance to the officers as in bootlegging cases, simply because the men arrested know that they will get no public or newspaper support if they attack or kill the officer of the law. But let resistance be made to a prohibition agent in the lawful performance of his duty and there is an immediate rallying to the defense of the bootlegger by those who are opposed to prohibition enforcement. Are we losing our sense of proportion when the arrest involves liquor?

I condemn without qualification unjustified use of firearms in the enforcement of the prohibition law, as well as any other law, but I think no one who is fair-minded will disagree with this editorial statement of *The Los Angeles Times:*

There seems to be a good deal of overemphasis for wet propaganda purposes of such regrettable affairs as the slaying of Jacob Hanson at Niagara Falls and of Henry Virkhula at International Falls, Minn. If either man had been killed by a policeman who mistook him for a burglar, the case would have been dismissed, so far as national public interest is concerned, in a few lines of the press, and it is inconceivable that it could have become a subject for Congressional discussion.

Who Is to Blame?

In expressing my condemnation of the use of unnecessary and unjustified violence in the name of prohibition enforcement I have the woman's privilege of saying, "I told you so."

I had not been in charge of prosecutions under the prohibition law more than a few months before I discovered what many people since have acknowledged: that hundreds of prohibition agents had been appointed through political pull and were as devoid of honesty and integrity as the bootlegging fraternity. I found that there were scores of prohibition agents no more fit to be trusted with a commission to enforce the laws of the United States and to carry a gun than the notorious bandit Jesse James. Among the evidences of this fact that early reached me was this letter from a judge known throughout the country as an upright, fearless, able jurist:

More intelligence ought to be used in selecting prohibition agents. The majority of them in my district are stupid, and on the witness stand under cross-examination conducted by highly paid and able lawyers for the bootleggers, they crumple up.

In my court room an agent testified that between the 17th of October and the 1st of November, about fourteen days, he drank 700 glasses of alcohol and 700 glasses of moonshine whiskey. That was a period of 14 days, and when 1,400 is divided by 14, it will be reasonably clear that he did not drink any such quantity. But if he only drank a fraction of that amount it would be sufficient to destroy his usefulness. The situation cannot be permitted to go much further because the judges are losing confidence in the integrity and veracity of the government's witnesses.

It was my opinion in 1921, and it still is, that the government is committing a crime against the public generally when it pins the badge of police authority on and hands a gun to a man of uncertain character, limited intelligence, or without giving systematic training for the performance of duties that involve the rights and possibly the lives of citizens.

The Untouchables

Eliot Ness with Oscar Fraley

Widespread police corruption in big cities like Chicago was not uncommon during Prohibition. It became standard practice for bootleggers to factor payoffs into their overhead. Everyone from the lowly cop on the beat to the police commissioner demanded a cut. For crime bosses like Al Capone, who ran a citywide operation, payoffs to government officials amounted to millions of dollars.

A few dedicated agents and policemen like Eliot Ness could not be bought for any price. Ness's Prohibition unit had been dubbed "untouchable" by the press because of their incorruptibility. The following selection is taken from Ness's biography. In it he describes one of many raids his unit would make that would cripple Capone's bootlegging business in Chicago. Despite their success as a unit, the Untouchables were disbanded after repeal. Ness became the director of public safety in Cleveland, Ohio, and later accepted an appointment as director of social protection, under the government Defense, Health, and Welfare section. Ness left government service in 1944 and became head of the Diebold Safe Company in Ohio. He died in 1957 of a heart attack before his book was published.

B eer was practically nonexistent in Chicago when we struck our greatest blow at the syndicate by uncovering a gigantic alcohol plant worth a quarter of a million dollars and turning out twenty thousand gallons a day.

So tremendous was this operation that the output not only

was shipped in carload lots of fifty-gallon drums but was pumped directly into railroad tank cars.

The tip came through an anonymous telephone call.

"I'd like to speak to Mr. Ness," a lady's voice said.

"This is he."

"Mr. Ness," she began, "I'm not going to give you my name, but I think maybe I have something that can help you. My husband told me that he heard from somebody that there is something funny going on in the plant of the Illinois Iron Company in the 1800 block on Diversey Avenue. They seem to think that maybe somebody is making beer or whiskey or something there."

"What makes them think so?" I asked.

"Well, I don't know," she said. "That's why I'm telling you to find out. It's about time somebody made this a decent city for us sober, hard-working people, and I just think you ought to look into it. So see that you do."

With that, she slammed the phone down in my ear.

We had received a number of anonymous tips as the months went by, some good and some completely unfounded. But none of them was overlooked; in each case, I, myself, or one of my men, would make a discreet but thorough check before we decided whether or not to conduct a raid.

I told [Marty] Lahart about the woman who had called and asked him to accompany me on a tour of inspection.

Casing the Joint

We drove out Diversey [Street] and finally came to the plant; a large sign proclaimed it to be the Illinois Malleable Iron Company. The huge six-story building looked exactly as advertised. I directed Marty to park in front of the building while I walked inside to take a close look.

A wide counter and, behind it, a number of women clerical workers indicated that this was a legitimate operation. When one of the women approached, I smiled innocently and asked:

"Could you tell me where the Lahart Lamp Factory is located?"

There being no such company in Chicago, as far as I knew, I was certain that the young lady couldn't tell me. But my intention was to lure her into conversation.

"No," she puzzled thoughtfully, "I don't believe I ever heard of it. Do you know the address?"

I told her I thought it was in the 1800 block on Diversey.

"No," she said positively, "It isn't around here or I would know about it."

"Are you sure?" I asked. "Have you worked here long?"

"I certainly am sure," she bridled. "I've been here three years and I know this whole neighborhood."

"I'm sorry, I didn't mean to offend you," I smiled. "Why, I didn't even know they employed pretty girls in an iron plant."

She simpered and, looking around, I observed in pseudo amazement:

"This certainly is a big place. Do they make iron all the way up to the top of the building? And if so, how do they get it down?"

"Oh, no," she replied. "Our company just uses the first four floors. There's another firm on the two top floors and they make paint—or something. But they've only been up there a few months.

"Well," I told her, "thanks a lot for your help. I guess I'd better get looking for that lamp company."

As I left the building, I saw an adjoining door. There was no name lettered on it and I found that it was locked.

"There's something peculiar there," I observed, back in the car. "If it is a legitimate paint company, that might explain our anonymous tipster's olfactory suspicion that they were making alcohol. Then, too, it seems improbable that such an obviously legitimate firm as Illinois Iron would permit a still to be operated on its premises. And, to boot, how would whoever is running the still get the stuff down?". . .

Finding the Evidence

During "bootleg hours," long after dark, Marty and I drove out Diversey again and parked about two blocks from the plant. We had planned to approach it from the rear, but stumbling down a spur track of the North Western Railroad tracks, we saw a bright light beaming in the rear of the building and were forced to retreat. Our only course was to approach it from the front, and as we did we saw lights in the windows on the upper two floors.

"I'm going up that fire escape," I told Marty. "If they're honest, we shouldn't get into any trouble. If they're not, trouble's what we're looking for, anyhow."

Marty boosted me up until I could catch the counterbalance which dropped the ladder. As I swung it down, the rusty iron made a tremendous screech. Breathlessly we waited, fearful that the noise might have been heard, but when nobody appeared I whispered to Marty:

"Here we go!"

Up we climbed, taking great care to move quietly; the rusted railings tore at our clothes and stained our hands. I swore softly as a jagged piece punctured the palm of my hand, but forgot the pain as my eyes drew level with the fifth-floor window sill and I looked into the lighted room within.

What I had smelled while climbing those last few yards had not been paint. And what I was looking at was not paint-manufacturing apparatus.

It was a giant alcohol still whose columns rose forty feet into the air and stretched through a hole cut into the ceiling or floor, depending on how you looked at it, between the fifth and sixth floors.

"Wow!" Marty breathed softly into my ear, "Would you take a look at that!"

It was by far the largest still either of us had ever seen, and we classed ourselves as experts in that department.

This was a mammoth operation, I realized as I watched six men working busily at various tasks in a floor space that stretched one hundred and twenty-five feet in both length and width. Two men operated an electrical lift, which was similar to that used in grain elevators. From the ground they hoisted large sacks of what I suspected to be corn sugar, used in the making of mash, and on the return trip to the railroad siding below they lowered an endless chain of loaded fifty-gallon drums.

I had seen enough. Now I wanted to get away before we were discovered. . . .

The Raid

The next day we laid our plans carefully, bringing the whole group in on the raid. Each man drew an exact assignment, because we had long since learned to leave nothing to chance. This time, of course, with the plant high up on the fifth and sixth floors, we could not use our favored method of smashing through the doors in our truck.

We arranged it so that Marty and I would go up the fire escape and be in position to enter through the windows at the appointed time. I assumed that there would be both a freight elevator and stairs in the back, so Seager, Leeson, Robsky, King and Cloonan were detailed to approach from the rear while Gardner, Chapman and Friel attacked from the front.

"Sam," I told Seager, "you and Leeson take the freight elevator while Robsky and King move up the stairs. That leaves Barney to cover the back from the landing platform just in case there is a way out through the iron works."

They nodded and I turned to Chapman.

"Lyle," I said, "will crash the front door and take Friel up the stairs with him. Gardner will remain down front and cover there in case someone tries to get out through the iron works. Meanwhile, Marty and I will crack in from the windows on the fifth and sixth floors."

It was close to midnight—and I was thankful that there was no moon—when we approached the huge building and parked several blocks away. Then we split up, Seager leading his squad down a side street to the railroad spur and noiselessly beginning his infiltration so that at the designated time we could attack simultaneously.

This time Marty and I were equipped with a small ladder so that we would not have to use the squeaking fire escape ladder. Together with Gardner, Chapman and Friel, we approached the front cautiously. Gardner and Chapman melted into the shadows near by, safe from the eyes of any chance patrol, and after a hasty look to make certain that nobody was in the side court we whisked in, planted the ladder, and Marty and I began our cautious climb. As we gained the fire escape, Friel removed the ladder and disappeared with it into the street.

Once again Marty and I were climbing up those rusty stairs, encumbered this time with our sawed-off shotguns. It was two minutes to midnight when we reached the fifth-floor landing. Motioning Marty up to the sixth floor with a jerk of my thumb, I peered inside to make certain that he wasn't seen as he climbed quickly through the light glare from the window and reached the slatted iron perch above my head.

I could see my watch easily in the glare from the window, and as the hands closed together I stood up, whistled shrilly and smashed the window with a slashing blow of my shotgun. Up above I could hear Marty doing the same as I lowered my head, held my arms in front of my face and leaped through in a shower of glass to the floor inside.

Four men stood slack jawed and stunned as I covered them with the sawed-off shotgun and called:

"This is a federal raid. Don't make a move!"

They raised their hands and stood quietly as I advanced on them. Within seconds, Marty came down a flight of inside stairs, pushing a fifth man along with the barrel of his shotgun.

"That's all that's up on the sixth floor," he said.

Within a few minutes, Robsky and King came charging in, panting from their headlong dash up the stairs. Chapman and Friel were gasping, too, as they joined us from the front. There was a grinding noise from the freight elevator as it jolted to a stop.

"It's a lot easier this way," Seager said, flashing one of his rare smiles as he noticed the heaving chests of those who had to make it hurriedly on foot. Leeson leaned against the back of the cage easily and nodded his agreement, his sawed-off shotgun trained on the white-faced elevator operator.

Taking Inventory

Now, with plenty of time to take a full inventory, I saw that this, without doubt, was the most staggering setup I had ever seen. The giant still was geared to turn out the almost unbelievable total of twenty thousand gallons a day. Certainly this amount couldn't be moved in fifty-gallon drums.

Lahart solved that puzzle when he called me to the back end of the vast room.

"Look here," he whistled, "pipes which must lead right to those tank cars on the siding."

That's exactly what they were, and further investigation disclosed that there also was an entire carload of empty fifty-gallon drums waiting below to be unloaded. A series of tremendous vats on the upper floor contained the amazing total of one hundred and twenty thousand gallons of mash.

There was another innovation, we discovered as we made an inventory. Up until this time, corn sugar had been the basic product used to make alcohol mash. But the mob on this operation had discovered a new and more efficient material, the mash for this giant still being made from hydrol, a mixture of grain and sugar.

Subsequent investigation disclosed that the still had been in operation almost six months without the workers in the iron company below ever becoming suspicious. I often wondered whether the mysterious female tipster was one of the women working downstairs. However, regardless of who she was, she had done us a tremendous favor. Estimating that approximately four hundred and eighty thousand gallons of alcohol had been shipped from the plant, with each gallon bringing the mob two dollars profit, we came to the conclusion that they had netted close to one million dollars in that brief period of operation.

This was another backbreaking blow to the mob's financial situation. They would sorely miss the lucrative income they had been receiving from the cooker in the sky.

A Small-Time Crook

Rafer Dooley

> Before Prohibition, robbery, gambling, extortion, rackets, and pimping were the chief criminal trades. But none of them had as much potential as bootlegging, which is why most of the underworld wanted to get involved in the production and sale of liquor during Prohibition. The cities were where the biggest bootleg operations were. Rival gangs fought over territory in which to distribute the illegal beverage. Expanding the business was a matter of "rubbing out" the boss of the rival gang. In the following selection, up-and-coming hood "Barefoot" Rafer Dooley recalls how dangerous it was in the big cities. Although it seemed like a romantic lifestyle, it was also a dangerous one for anybody who showed weakness.

I come from Tennessee. I run away from home with my older brother Ben. My folks were ignorant, illiterate hillbillies, but they tried to push me through school. I quit when I was fourteen, and Ben and me we come to St. Louis. I took whatever menial jobs I could find there and elsewhere around the country. I had the wanderlust in me, and I put it into effect. Most kids of that age can't. I was a dishwasher at a lumber camp. I started boxing and so forth until I articulated back to St. Louis.

I got to know a lot of the boys in St. Louis. I knew Dinty Colfax, who headed up what later come to be called the Egan Rats. He had a saloon, a hangout for the boys. The names that come from that are too numerous to mention. You could

Excerpted from *Ardent Spirits: The Rise and Fall of Prohibition*, by John Knobler (New York: G.P. Putnam's Sons, 1973). Copyright © 1973 by John Knobler. Reprinted with permission.

go on into the night—Fred "Killer" Burke,[1] Gus Winkler, Johnny Moore, Buddy Eppensheimer—on and on. I'd deliver messages for Dinty when he didn't want to use the phone. I would also deliver liquor for him to selected customers. I became known as trustworthy. I am working wherever I can work, and I am stealing whenever I have to steal.

I'd already been in Mexico—Tijuana—and I began running whiskey across the border into California. It wasn't as complicated then as it later turned out to be. For a small stipend [bribe] the guard would look the other way, and you just drove your pickup truck past him.

A Rough Start

I organized a bunch of constituents [associates] in Los Angeles. I made contact there again with my brother Ben. He's going much stronger than I am, so he fit me in with some of his operations which consisted of hijacking whiskey. We had some bad scrapes, and it looked as though we were going to get killed in California because we interfered with stronger mobs than us.

There never was a hijacking without a tipoff, you understand. I mean it would be impossible. Well, the gambling czar of Los Angeles at this time I'm telling about, in 1922 or '23, was Farmer Page [Milton B. "Farmer" Page, an L.A. gangster killed in 1925], and he was in liquor too. One of his drivers told his girlfriend where he was going to collect a load of whiskey off a boat—in a little town that sits right on the ocean, adjacent to Long Beach. She happened to be a better girlfriend of my brother than she was of the driver. She revealed the information, so naturally we went in force with sawed-off shotguns, eight or ten of us. Numbers would be the thing that would dissuade you from resistance. We waited till they loaded the truck. Then we merely told them to get out of the truck, that we were taking over. No harsh words. We didn't harm them. We just drove off and left them as is.

1. One of the gunmen hired by Al Capone for the St. Valentine's Day massacre

We had a drop for the whiskey with another competitor of Page's. We had the whiskey sold before we stole it. He paid us $5,000, a lot of money at the time when eggs cost a dime a dozen and you could buy a new Ford for $350—a different monetary system than you have today. My cut was 10 percent.

It became known that it was us that did it. There was a confrontation, and quite a few of my brother's constituents fell and became deceased on the spot.

Ben branched out from hijacking into the heist. He was unsuccessful, and they sent him to San Quentin for ten years. I articulated back to Chicago. Having performed with the Egan Rats, some of whom had moved there from St. Louis, I arrived with good credentials, extremely good credentials, though I was only a neofate [neophyte] of eighteen. Nowadays a guy eighteen, with his long hair, you wouldn't pay him no more mind than a billy goat.

A Piece of the Action

At this time, if I'm not exaggerating, there were about ten mobs in Chicago. There was the Irish North Side mob under Deanie O'Banion, the O'Connell mob on the West Side, Joe Saltis and Frankie McErlane on the South Side—oh, dear God, never has there been such tough guys. The North Side mob gave me and my constituents, about twenty-five of them, a district, an allocation, five blocks square. This was our reward for faithful service in the past. With it went the right to distribute beer and whiskey. Of course, you had to protect your territory. You couldn't call for help. If you couldn't handle it yourself, you lost it. That was the law. So when you were infringed upon, you had to retaliate immediately, or you didn't have nothing left.

It was a nightclub district, full of bars, handbooks, crap games, gambling joints. It seemed as though every wise-guy heist artist, mechanic, con man and burglar gaviated [gravitated] to our district. We worked hard for their patronage, and we reached some affluence, but easy come, easy go and all that.

I met muscle with muscle trying to defend my equity, and I got hurt. I was shot several times. In fact, I was cut all to pieces. The worst fight was with some characters who figured that if they eliminated me, they could take over the territory easy. That was unavailing. They didn't fare well at all.

Networking with Scarface

I had a close immediate contact with Al Capone in about 1926. He urinated on my shoes. It happened in the men's room of the Croydon Hotel. He was drunk, and I was drunk. He didn't know who I was, but I knew him. I had the reputation of being the most vicious left-hook puncher in Chicago, that's the God's truth. We were on the verge of slugging it out when Al thought better of it. He didn't exactly apologize, but he admitted to a social error. I decided to overlook the indiscretion. We had a drink and whenever he saw me around town after that, it was "Hello, kid, how you doing?"

Capone was cunning as a fox, but he didn't have the balls of the Irish gangsters like Deanie O'Banion, not the kind it takes to walk into a bank and make an unsecured loan at the end of a .38 pistol.

I was pinched [arrested] at least a hundred times, but they made the charge stick only once. That was when I paid a return visit to California in 1927. They accused me of robbery. There was this rodeo, and it's alleged that me and some associates heisted the cash box. I laid in jail for a year. The experience showed me I was just a neofate [neophyte], after all, and it taught me to improve my *modus operandi* [way of operating].

As soon as I got out, I articulated back to Chicago. I never again fell into the toils of the law. Nevertheless, I became discouraged. The rewards were getting less and less. Too many of my constituents were being killed or landing in jail. Maybe I was luckier or maybe more sagacious. I decided to quit the rackets.

They say crime don't pay. You tell that to the real higher-archery [hierarchy] of crime and they'll laugh theirselves into nervous hysteria. It don't pay only if you're apprehended. The saying is a misnomer used to dissuade youthful offenders from progressing into criminology. If the venture succeeds, like when me and my constituents were distributing liquor on the North Side, it pays fine, very fine indeed.

Rumrunners

Anonymous

One of the toughest crimes to fight during Prohibition was rum-running. Anybody with a boat could make a fast buck by smuggling alcohol in from Canada or the Bahamas (it was still legal to purchase alcohol there) to the United States. It is estimated that more than a million gallons of alcohol crossed into the country from Canada alone, by land and sea. There were not enough customs officials or Coast Guard cutters to cover the entire coastline and border. Nevertheless, rumrunners were caught or killed daily trying to outrun patrols. To the rumrunner, the risks were worth it, especially after 1929 when the Great Depression had put so many people out of work. The following selection is a firsthand account by the unnamed officer of a ship that was seized for rum-running.

I was in the rum-running business for a couple of years, off and on. It was the only dollar you could make; they were only paying $35 to $40 a month in the three-masted coasters. I was in five schooners and some steamers that ran rum. They paid us in wages and bonus. A deckhand got $75 a month and $75 bonus. I was mate and got $150 a month and $150 bonus. The Diamantina was built in Lunenburg; she was a new vessel, had a crew of ten or 11, and would carry 6,000 cases. Really, they weren't cases; there were six bottles to a bag, sewed up in a diamond-shaped burlap package.

In St. Pierre, gin was 25 cents a quart, imported champagne, $1 a bottle, rum, 50 cents a gallon. The rum people owned the warehouses at St. Pierre. The stuff they had was Black and White, White Label, Smugglers, and lots of im-

Excerpted from *The Black Ship: Rumrunners of Prohibition*, by Everett S. Allen (Boston: Little, Brown and Company, 1965). Copyright © 1965 by Everett S. Allen. Reprinted by permission of the publisher.

ported champagne. They used to get the liquor from Europe in wooden cases and they put the stuff in burlap there, because it was easier to stow and handle. There's no wood on St. Pierre and when they got mountains of those wooden liquor boxes, the people there shingled their barns and fish shacks with them and used the stuff for kindling. The rum people built up St. Pierre, warehouses and everything.

We'd get clearance at St. Pierre to go to Nassau, with a load or in ballast. Some boats had their cargoes consigned, but some didn't. There were a lot at it in the peak of the business, maybe a hundred steamers and schooners. Sometimes we'd get a load from a European steamer; those big steamers would carry 60,000 to 70,000 cases and they'd anchor about 30 miles offshore of New York. Intermediate vessels, such as I was on, would go out there and take 5,000 to 6,000 cases and go in to anchor on Rum Row.

Cash and Carry Business

We had all kinds of customers. There were lobster traps out there, so the lobstermen would come out from Sheepshead Bay, and the scallopers, too. We used to sell small lots, as well as 600 to 800 cases to a boat. We took cash. Some of them came in speedboats. One boat had false gas tanks in behind the bulwarks [the side of a boat above the upper deck]; unscrew the covers, the top came off the split tanks and he could take about twenty cases.

Sometimes we carried supercargoes [designated official in charge of cargo]. They would notify the charterers when we left St. Pierre and give us the position to anchor. They'd come off and we'd retail it. Sometimes there would be six or seven to as many as twenty boats alongside. Lobstermen would put down a couple of cases; little fishing boats would carry in two or three. One fellow took two–three cases and he came out every good-weather day and peddled the stuff on a bicycle in Brooklyn.

Some of them weren't even boatmen. They'd come out with an oil hat and oil skins, but wearing dress shoes. They couldn't handle a boat and they'd come at you, bang, head on. They followed the garbage scows out to find us and we'd show them on the compass how to get back. They'd come alongside, ask you what you had—sometimes some of it was on deck—and you'd tell him the price and he'd pay you. Then you give orders to the crew and say, "Give this fellow so many of this, so many of that—"

Once in a while maybe some of the stuff broke in the burlap but I never once saw any go overboard. When you're at it all the time, you get used to it. We were young. We took it off the big ships with a cargo net, but a case is nothing to handle when you're used to it. And when the owners would come, say to get 400 to 500 cases, they'd match their half of a torn playing card with our half. Once in a while, if we had liquor in wooden boxes, the customers would put it in sacks themselves if they were going to dump it in the water with a buoy inshore.

Offshore, we'd move around. The Coast Guard was hanging around and we'd watch them. They'd shut off their lights. It was a cutter that took in the Diamantina and the steamer [Sagatind] that we were getting a load from. The way it was, you never knew who you was working for. This fellow was supercargo. He had sold to this boat [the Coast Guard test boat] and they had marked the money. Now if he had burned it or given it to the crew, he would have been all right. But they had bought ten or twenty cases or something like that, and he had to open the safe—he had taken in about $6,000—and the marked money proved that you had made a connection, you had sold booze.

An Official Piece of the Action

When we anchored off the Statue of Liberty, the customs fellows came aboard. In no time at all, they wanted to get at the whisky. They told us they could get a good market for it, but we didn't want nothing to do with them. Every evening, they came out with suitcases, one fellow at the head of ten or twelve, the watch at night. They packed their little grips with three or four bottles.

After the hearing was over, we went down to a Brooklyn

dock and our fellows would carry three–four bottles ashore, maybe to buy a suitcase or a shirt and when they got to the head of the dock, the guards wouldn't let them out without paying; maybe if they started out with four bottles, they'd get out with one or two.

We had rifles and so on aboard; I had a beautiful repeater shotgun. They just took it and I couldn't get it back. I tried, but I couldn't. They said they were breaking up the whisky; I never saw them break up none, but I saw them take plenty

Smugglers' Chanty

Author of The Black Ships, *Everett S. Allen grew up in a New England coastal town and knew people involved in rum-running. Most of them were not gangsters and criminals. They were fishermen and boat owners who saw an opportunity to make a little money and have an adventure. To them, rum-running hailed back to a more colorful time when pirates sailed the high seas and raided the coasts. "The Smugglers' Chanty" was written by Allen's father and reflects this attitude shared by many in the coastal communities.*

"Oh, we don't give a damn for our old Uncle Sam
    Way-o, whisky and gin!
Lend us a hand when we stand in to land
Just give us time to run the rum in."

From sunny southern island ports
That dot the Spanish Main,
A brand new gang of pirate sports
Have put to sea again.

But differing from men of old
Who counted all fair prey
These modern pirates gain their gold
In quite a different way.

Unto our unprotected shores
Forbidden rum they bring
Patrol boats chase them by the scores
But still the pirates sing:

ashore. The ones who made the most money out of it were the customs officers and the policemen, because it never cost them anything.

There was an awful lot of graft going on with the charters, the hijacking, the police and the Coast Guard payoffs. The Coast Guard got to catching the inshore rum boats, then they'd put men aboard, and come offshore to buy from us. That's how they got the Diamantina. Once, we saw them catch a boat in the daytime. By and by, when it got dark, we

---

"Oh, schooners and steamers and cruisers and all
Way-o, whisky and gin!
Chase us with cutters and battleships tall
Still we have time to bring the rum in."

And so it goes, our agents grow
More haggard every day
They form new plans each week or so
But nothing works their way.

They spread wild rumors round about
That all the booze is dope
But even this doesn't help them out
And they are losing hope.

Each day they claim "The peak is passed,
The job is well in hand,"
Each day we read "Rum fleet is massed
A few miles off the land."

Our laws are dry as dry can be
Although the land is moist
And jolly pirates out at sea
Chant loudly as they hoist:

"'Tis easy and free for us boys out at sea
Way-o, whisky and gin!
Pigs will all fly when the country goes dry
Give us the word, we'll run the rum in."

Everett S. Allen, *The Black Ships.* Boston: Little, Brown, 1965.

had a customer alongside; we had the tarpaulins up, and the first two tiers in—we had loaded about 400 cases aboard him and he was trying to beat me out. He was saying he didn't have as many cases as I knew he had. So I jumped aboard him; we had covered his stuff with canvas because otherwise the cases would show, and I was down there counting the cases.

Well, along came these Coast Guard fellows with the rum boat they had caught in the daytime. They jumped right aboard our customer, but they fell when they landed and that gave me a chance to get back aboard our vessel.

We paid those Coast Guards $1,500. I thought at first that was just to let our boat go. But they waited around while we finished loading it. They were cursing us up in the clouds while we loaded and they kept saying, "How long is it going to take you to load this damned thing?" I said, "You got yours; what's your complaint?" So they said the ship they were off had gone to Fire Island and would come back before daylight. For the $1,500, they were willing to give our boat safe passage in to the beach, but they had to get back out before their ship came back and they were afraid we wouldn't get through in time.

Between Us and Them

We were anchored, with our lights on, near Jones Inlet. There were a lot of us out there and a lot of passenger boats, coming and going, because it was near the ship lanes. The fellows in the inshore rum boats used us as shields. They were cute and they knew enough to keep for the ships going into New York.

Well, there was this boat going like hell, must be fifty miles an hour and too much speed for the cutter that was chasing him. The rum boat got on the other side of us from the cutter, used us as a shield and the cutter fired high through our rigging, figuring that would make him stop. But it didn't. After he used us for a shield, he got on the other side of a big vessel going into New York and by that time, the Coast Guard couldn't catch him anyhow.

Chapter 4

The General Public

Chapter Preface

The failure of Prohibition can be attributed to many causes. But perhaps the two most significant reasons were the public's indifference to breaking Prohibition laws and the change in social mores brought on by the roaring twenties. Because drinking was both illegal and yet acceptable to many people, it achieved a higher level of social legitimacy among men and women. Speakeasies were regarded as more chic than criminal to most people. This image was helped along by the patronage of celebrities, members of high society, and even royalty. The Prince of Wales, Edward VIII, was reported to have gone to a club owned by the infamous speakeasy proprietor Texas Guinan. Edward was almost caught when a police raid burst in during his visit. But Guinan quickly shuffled the prince into the kitchen, put a chef's hat on him and told him to cook eggs until things cooled off. The police never suspected.

Other regular patrons known to visit speakeasies were newspapermen, high-level politicians, and Prohibition agents who would drop by after work. And for the first time women also frequented drinking establishments alongside men. This was something that would have been frowned upon before Prohibition since proper women would never be openly seen drinking or in a bar. But the Victorian values of the past had been discarded for a more carefree lifestyle. The speakeasy especially appealed to young people who were attracted to the speakeasies' rebellious allure. They might never have been drawn to alcohol if it were not for Prohibition. Some historians believe the speakeasy changed the lifestyle of an entire generation in this manner.

If You Don't Like the Law, Break It

Corey Ford

> One of the main reasons Prohibition failed was because of
> widespread civil disobedience by the general public. Many
> citizens, even self-proclaimed "drys," continued to frequent
> bars and purchase alcohol for their own use. Corey Ford was
> an American sporting writer who vehemently opposed Prohi-
> bition. In the following article, which appeared in the May
> 1930 *Vanity Fair,* Ford advises his readers to continue to
> break the law. Ford urges his audience to join his Anti-
> Speakeasy League, an organization devoted to repealing Pro-
> hibition laws in order to rid the land of the "necessary evil" of
> speakeasies and the exorbitant prices they can charge for
> liquor. The satiric humor of Ford's plea to join the fictitious
> league was not lost on those who had witnessed the power of
> the Anti-Saloon League in lobbying for the passage of the
> national Prohibition laws.

Several months ago there were smuggled into this country three and one half cases of excellent liquor. These included Scotch, Rye, Rum, some Sherry and some Sauterne.

Now, I should like nothing better than to admit here that
I smuggled these goods into this country myself. I should
not care to reveal what my procedure was, to be sure; for the
very last thing I should wish to do would be to assist the
Government in any way in its attempt to enforce this Eighteenth Amendment. But at least I should welcome the op-

portunity of stating in print that I had broken the Prohibition Law, that I am an active conscientious objector to this Law, that I do not consider an infraction of this particular Law to be a crime, and that I fully intend to repeat my offense again and again.

Unfortunately my lawyers are more expedient. In this country, so they inform me, it is illegal to break the law. To my great surprise, and doubtless to the surprise of the reader, we are popularly supposed still to be a nation of law-abiding people; and if I were to confess in print that I had broken the Eighteenth Amendment, I should be liable to arrest and prosecution, and the courageous magazine that published my confession would be barred ignominiously from the mails.

Well; I am no more of a fool than the rest of my countrymen. I must bow to superior authority. When I break the law, I suppose, I must do it under cover of secrecy, like everyone else. In this case, therefore, I will state that the incident which I describe is entirely fictitious, that all the characters in this fable are purely imaginary, and that the whole scene is laid in a mythical Democracy on the dark side of the moon.

A "Fictional" Account

Very well, then. Several months ago there were smuggled into this country three and one half cases of entirely imaginary liquor. These included Scotch, Rye, Rum, some Sherry and some Sauterne.

As a matter of fact, the entirely imaginary character who accomplished this entirely imaginary feat did not even find the adventure very exciting. There were no shouts in the dark, no bloody scuffle, no hail of bullets from a Coast Guard riot-gun. He did not even need to hide his identity behind a series of bright colored beards, change his name to Brookhart [Iowa Senator (1922–1933) Smith Wildman Brookhart], or even pretend that he was deaf and dumb and thus enter the country disguised as a United States Senator. His process merely involved the cooperation of a gentleman actively engaged in the bootlegging profession—a gentleman, by the by, who recently resigned in disgust from Uncle Sam's own Coast Guard, reformed, and became a rum-runner. Through this gentleman's advice and encouragement, he was enabled to bring his contraband goods through the blockade, repack them in suitcases, transport them to New York in the compartment of a train, and run them without incident from the railway station to his home in an ordinary, or fifteen-and-five, taxicab.

The point is that, in order to be able to offer his guests a highball or a glass of wine a trifle more pure than the highball or the glass of wine which he would otherwise have purchased here in America, our entirely imaginary character disobeyed an Amendment to the Constitution, broke twenty incidental statutes, betrayed the President of his country, committed an outrage upon the person of Civic Virtue, spat on the flag, yanked the tail feathers from the American eagle, and trampled Law, Patriotism and Stephen Decatur into the dust.

And at least I can say here—at the risk of being censored—that if I had by any possible chance been this entirely imaginary character, it would have been the proudest moment of my civic career.

Drinking in Protest

For it just happens that I cannot be a hypocrite. I am temperamentally unable to mumble obedience to a law which I am in fact disobeying every day. I cannot, like so many millions of the citizens of these benighted States, drink wet and vote dry. I cannot quite resign myself to that general dull apathy in which the patriots of our hinterland, merely because they can get to drink what they want when they want it, are content to sip in silence and let well enough alone. Myself, I like to feel that every drink I take is a worthy gesture in a worthy cause; that every time I break the Prohibition Law I am perhaps making it just that bit weaker. I have broken the law many times; I shall break it again, and again, and again, so long as it remains upon the books; but I break it primarily because such an infraction is our only weapon of protest today.

I break this law because I am convinced it is morally obscene.

And those persons who have unbounded faith in America—and I am afraid I am not one of them—may find some slight basis for their optimism in the fact that this same spirit of revolt is spreading slowly but surely among our very young. The members of this generation rather feel that their elders have sold them short. The Prohibition Law, insulting their own powers of self-determination and self-discipline, was put over on them by a group of weaklings who needed a moral truss themselves and who were therefore unwilling to trust their children to walk without aid. By a curious coincidence, despite its crude upbringing in an age of speak-easies, hip flasks and drunken women, this Younger Generation is at heart passionately for Temperance. They desire, of course, some sensible regulation of the liquor traffic—some Quebec or Bratt system—because that seems to them temperate and just. To be temperate and to be just is their entire crusade. They over-drink today—and they will continue to over-drink as long as this legal restraint is on them—but they are not drunkards; they break the law, as I do, but they do it proudly, defiantly, honestly.

We do not want to break the law. We only request the simple privilege of governing our private lives and working out our private destinies in our own bungling way. We want the privilege of making our own moral choices. We do not want the old-fashioned saloon any more than we want the modern speakeasy; but we want legislative meddling with our morals even less. We only ask to be let alone.

We do not seek to legislate the private habits of the Drys. If they choose not to drink, that is their personal concern. We do not ask that they approve of our drinking; we do not even ask them to associate with us when we drink; we only request that they mind their own business, and we will mind ours. It is not necessary for people to agree exactly in their private tastes in order to live amicably together. We doubt very much, for example, whether Jack Spratt [Mother Goose character] and his wife would have got along one-tenth as well with their married life if Mrs. Spratt had suddenly taken it into her head that fat was the only possible food, and had passed an Amendment to the Constitution forbidding her husband to eat lean.

Just Break the Law

We break the law only because it happens to be our sole means of reiterating this defiance of legislative interference. We are a little weary of repeating facts. Fanatic Drys—and there is Methodism in their madness—do not want to hear facts. Arguments of the universal failure of Prohibition—the cocktail parties, the college brawls, the applejack in Pennsylvania and the corn-whiskey in Kentucky, the home-brewed beer in Kansas and the grapes in California, the nation-wide breakdown of respect and honour—all these fall on deaf ears; they are immediately licked and slithered over with the slimy, healing platitudes of "economic necessity" and "comfort" and "prosperity." We are told and retold that oldest saw: "Prohibition is a noble experiment." We are handed gruesome chromos of the old-fashioned saloon, as though the modern speakeasy were not ten times more vicious. Small wonder that we are discouraged. Small wonder that we cease talking, and resort instead to action.

Personally, I should like to call on every free-thinking American of my generation, and every American of the older generation who can think at all, to break this law; break it repeatedly; break it whenever he can. Drink what you please, when you please. Urge others to drink. Don't betray the bootleggers who are smuggling liquor for you. In every way possible flaunt your defiance of the Eighteenth Amendment. Render it inoperative. Ignore it, abrogate it, wipe it out. *Whilst it stands there, let it be disobeyed.*

Our Lives Are Our Own

I suppose I am a fanatic myself; because I cannot tolerate the smug, sententious statements of the fanatic Drys. There is nothing which irritates me more profoundly than the spectacle of an elderly gentleman who, because of his preeminence in the field of science or manufacture or big business, takes unto himself the role of spiritual adviser to a nation. The fact that a man has invented an electric light bulb, or manufactured an inexpensive automobile, or been elected the Chief Executive of a nation, does not of necessity make him an authority upon the moral health of his fellow-men. Be he ever so successful in his profession, still my private life is none of his business.

Mr. [Thomas] Edison, for example, I have no doubt is a dear old man, utterly out of touch with the world, doubtless without even a very clear idea of what his publicity directors are sending out about him each day. It would be silly to suggest that Mr. Edison is not worthy of our greatest respect—as a scientist. But when he feels that his scientific achievements give him the prerogative to employ this well-earned respect in an attempt to influence (as he unfortu-

Purposes of the Anti-Speakeasy League

Whereas: We, the undersigned, are convinced that the modern Speakeasy, with its poisonous liquor, its exorbitant prices, and its free access to women, constitutes a blot and a stain upon our American civilization; and,

Whereas: Such a source of temptation, vice and corruption is a far greater menace to the morality of this nation than its comparatively innocent predecessor, the Saloon; and,

Whereas: We feel that this obnoxious Speakeasy, with all its attendant evils, could only exist under the Eighteenth Amendment to the Constitution;

Now, therefore, be it resolved: That the Anti-Speakeasy League is founded to fight this corruption and protect our children from the baleful influence of the Speakeasy, by uniting to destroy this Prohibition Law under which the Speakeasy flourishes; and,

That we do deplore and condemn as un-American and dangerous to the morals of our children, for their support of the disgraceful Speakeasy, the obsolete and outmoded Anti-

nately can) the moral choice of a hundred million people, then I wish dear old Mr. Edison would invent a device to keep his own mouth closed.

And when Mr. [Henry] Ford (no relation of mine, may I rather plaintively urge), a well-known manufacturer and business executive, capitalizes the excessive publicity which his product and consequently his name have received, and endeavors thereby to dictate your morals and mine, I rather feel that Mr. Ford is forgetting his place as a private citizen. What notoriety Mr. Ford's name has attained was not earned through any conspicuous success in the field of social welfare. He is famed primarily for his cars, not for his prowess as a philosopher. And if Mr. Ford's reiterated statement that Prohibition is a success can overlook so completely the acknowledged fact that his own manufacturing town of Dear-

---

Saloon League, the Women's Christian Temperance Union, the Methodist Board of Temperance, Prohibition and Public Morals, the Women's National Committee for Law Enforcement, Mrs. Ella Boole, Mr. Henry Ford, Mr. Thomas Edison, Mr. Andrew Volstead, Senators Brookhart, Borah, and Jones, Mr. F. Scott McBride, Mr. Clarence True Wilson, and all other public or private citizens who contribute to the current reign of vice, corruption and drunkenness by their misguided fealty to an immoral and impracticable law; and finally,

That we, the Anti-Speakeasy League, do urge all our members to fight the Speakeasy, and its aforementioned supporters, by constant petitions to Congress, by our refusal to cooperate with the present odious Law, and by a complete campaign of conscientious objection to the Eighteenth Amendment, in order to restore the ideal of Temperance to these benighted States.

(Signed) _____

(Mail this blank to *Vanity Fair*, Graybar Building, New York)

"The Anti-Speakeasy League," *Vanity Fair,* May 1930.

born is at present soaking wet, I cannot see how his current statements on the subject are any more valuable than his other imbecile experiment with the destinies of humanity, when he launched his famous Peace Ship during the war. [Henry Ford opposed WWI and sent a boat full of pacifists to Europe to try and negotiate peace.]

Mr. Ford incidentally has stated that if Prohibition is ever repealed he will stop making cars and retire; which I happen to consider the most effective argument in favor or repealing Prohibition that I have heard yet.

President Hoover Is Not a Moral Authority

And finally when Mr. Hoover, the elected Chief Executive of the United States, goes on record as saying that it is a citizen's "moral obligation" to support the Eighteenth Amendment, then I can only exclaim with Dr. John A. Ryan, a well-known professor of sociology: "He is no more a moral authority than I am. Let him not lay down dogmatically the law that good citizens should tell others what they should do. The President is no supreme arbiter of the moral duty of men."

This bigotry, these sententious utterances by men who cannot mind their own business, all this tall talk of moral obligations and patriotic citizenship, has served to disgust the younger generation with the Prohibition Amendment; but nothing has succeeded in fanning the flame of revolt among them more violently than the activities of the men entrusted with the task of enforcing the law. The indiscriminate shootings, the killing of innocent citizens by bungling Coast Guardsmen, the unwarranted search of private homes, the sinking of foreign ships and utter disregard for the first principles of international courtesy, the scrapping of every law both of government and of humanity, all these things have aroused in the younger hearts an utmost sense of shame for their country and their flag.

All this is not hearsay. I am not merely an impressionable New Yorker swayed by the propaganda of a wet press. I have seen these things, and I know what I am talking about.

It so happened, during a recent vacation, that I was privileged to mingle intimately with a group of men actively engaged in the prosperous business of running liquor into this country. I talked with them, listened to their stories, watched them on one or two proud occasions load their boats; and I may say that I have never found a crowd of men more honest, more thoroughly decent, or less convinced that they were in any sense criminals.

Not that these men objected to the rather exorbitant rates which these Government Officials charged them for protection. They would willingly pay over one third of each load for the privilege of being winked through the lines; that seemed a trifle stiff, but they could adjust their prices in America to cover this added expense. But they did object mildly when the other two-thirds of their load was subsequently seized, when their boats were sunk and they were sent scurrying unceremoniously down the beach with bullets spattering about their heels, and when the entire load was later divided among the captors and not so much as one bottle ever officially recorded. They did object when their empty boats, tied peacefully along-shore in an off season, were seized without a trace of evidence aboard, summarily towed out, and burned; or when a youth in the full flush of his first uniform opened fire on them after they had halted unarmed; or when their crafts were picked up fifty miles offshore, in British waters, towed back within the twelve-mile limit, and then solemnly confiscated. These things, they felt, were not quite cricket.

There's a Government Double Standard

For example. A Long Key fishing guide, who did a little bootlegging now and then on a small scale, was apprehended and arrested near a small town on the coast of Florida, and presently brought up before the local magistrate. "You are accused of smuggling sixty cases of liquor into this country," said the judge sternly; "do you plead guilty?" "I do not," replied the culprit with some spirit. "I brought *one hundred* and sixty cases of liquor into this country, and I want to know what became of the other hundred cases." There was a moment of consternation, a hurried consultation, and the Judge pronounced the case dismissed. "And what's more," His Honor whispered ominously in the culprit's ear as he left the courtroom, "I advise you to clear out of this town as soon as possible."

For example, again. An elderly rum-runner, a retired sea-captain with a bright pink face and amiable blue eyes that had no malice in them as he spoke, related how he had saved up his profits for years until last season he could afford to purchase a specially-constructed speedboat with a twin-Liberty motor that could average fifty and outdistance with ease the usual Government cutter. At last his boat was finished; he journeyed upstate, paid for it, and ran the shiny new craft proudly down to Miami. Only once did his discretion desert him; while he was passing a Government boat on the way home, he could not resist the temptation to let it out a little and disappear down the bay in a fan of white spray. It was the following day that the Government agents discovered his new boat lying innocently at its dock, yet to make its first run; seized it without warrant; towed it out to sea, and nonchalantly blew it to pieces.

The Prohibitionist will doubtless say that this was perfectly just. The Agents had reason to be fairly certain that its owner was a bootlegger. He would in all likelihood use the boat at some time to break the law. The boat was a potential accessory to a crime; and they were justified in breaking the law of private property for the higher good of Prohibition.

Prohibition Is Subverting the Constitution

I think that is a rather dangerous principle. If such a procedure were universally adopted, then the logical course would be to ignore other laws as well. Slowly but surely we should bankrupt all law in order to enforce this one law. Already Chairman Wickersham has suggested in all seriousness the abolition of the traditional right of trial by jury. Already we have seen numerous instances of search without warrant. Tapping telephone wires for information is a common practice. Private property and private lives have been sacrificed without consideration for legal rights. The Prohibition Law is gradually scrapping item after item of the Bill of Rights. To get one apple, we are chopping down the whole tree.

I think the time has come to call for an honest definition of terms. There is no greater impudence in this country today than the titles which are flaunted with the blandest hypocrisy by the Prohibition Organizations and the leagues of Professional Drys. Such misnomers as the "Anti-Saloon League" or "The Women's Christian Temperance Union" or "The Methodist Board of Temperance, Prohibition and Public Morals" constitute an active insult to any decent intelligence. These names may have had some meaning once, when the organizations were still idealistic and young; today they are merely sheep's clothing which covers a profound prejudice and bigotry and renders the titles—and the organizations—obsolete.

Let us examine these terms, then, a little more closely. Let us ponder for the first time what they really mean. Logically every decent-thinking citizen would support an Anti-Saloon League. No one devoted to temperance desires to see the return of the Saloon. If the Anti-Saloon League lived up to its title, we should have no quarrel. But what do we find? The Saloon has gone, their main purpose is accomplished, their only possible function today is to stand around with the hose and guard the smouldering embers against any return of the blaze; but still they hang on, fighting desperately, no longer against the outlawed Saloon but against all temperance, reform, progress, and attempts to solve this national problem which their own stupid fanaticism has created.

And the Women's Christian Temperance Union? Nothing could sound more innocent. We all try to be Christian; we all want to be Temperate. Yet this organization, masquerading under a false front of tolerance, constitutes the most active enemy in America of what is sane, human and decent, and by its active opposition to all attempts at moderation it no more fulfills the purpose of Temperance than it deserves the title of Christian.

And the Methodist Board of Temperance, Prohibition and Public Morals? I have never seen four words more unhappily wedded. For every intelligent person knows that the medieval fanaticism of Methodism and the modern ideal of Temperance are irrevocably opposed, and have no more to do with each other than Prohibition has to do with Public Morals. (For that matter, I do not quite see what the *Methodists* have to do with Public Morals, excepting their own; but doubtless that is merely my lack of sympathy with the missionary spirit of the church militant.) Under such a confusion of terms, is it any wonder that the members of the Board themselves are the victims of a similar confusion of blind prejudices and hates.

The Anti-Speakeasy League

Well, the Younger Generation has a very simple remedy for it all. I have said that we are for Temperance. We have seen the Prohibition Law in America set back our cause a hundred years; and so we are roused to fight. And it is this generation, crusading passionately for Temperance in a world of fanatic Drys, that I should like to see united into one vast organization which we may call—in deference to its defunct predecessor—the Anti-Speakeasy League.

The purposes of this League are outlined in full elsewhere in this issue. It is, literally, an attempt to fight fire with fire; an effort if I may change my simile in mid-stream, to weigh down the other side of the scales in the hope that we may in time achieve the final balance of temperance. We shall pattern our activities on our illustrious predecessor, the Anti-Saloon League. Just as they are outraged by the corruption in those old-fashioned dens of vice, so we are outraged by the evils of the more modern saloons. We shall not ape them so far as to attempt to smash all speakeasies with hatchets—fortunately we are living today in a more enlightened age—but we shall attack the enemy no less violently at its source: The Eighteenth Amendment. There we shall concentrate our efforts. We shall endeavor in every way to fight this Amendment, either remove it or render it impotent and useless. It is only by killing the Prohibition Law that our Anti-Speakeasy League can accomplish its purpose.

There shall be no dues and no meetings in our Organization. We have no badge or button. We shall have but one obligation: it shall be the duty of each member to pledge himself to preserve and pass on to his children and his children's children a single word which has been almost forgotten in the United States since the Eighteenth Amendment: that obsolete word "liberty."

Mail your blanks in NOW.

The Parlor

Charles Angoff

The widespread casual disregard for the liquor laws surprised even "wet" supporters. After the passage of the Eighteenth Amendment, there were actually more places to get a drink than before liquor was declared illegal. This was especially true in the big cities where speakeasies could be easily hidden in backrooms and cellars. It is estimated New York had more than thirty thousand speakeasies during Prohibition.

There were many different kinds of speakeasies to choose from. They ranged from simple workingman's bars to lavish nightclubs that featured nightly shows with big name entertainment. Editor and critic Charles Angoff had his share of favorites. In the following selection Angoff remembers the places that were less like bars and more like salons in the European tradition. These salons or parlors, which did not exist before or after Prohibition, were havens where art and intellectualism flourished. Because of this highbrow atmosphere, Angoff considered them to be one of the only good things to come out of Prohibition.

M any people think all speakeasies were low, lurid, and immoral places, among the many evils of the twenties and thirties. Dens of iniquity. Cesspools of sin. Many, perhaps most, of them were just that. The food and the drink in them were truly dreadful. So was the clientele.

But there were other speakeasies that were charming places where men and women of breeding met. They were less drinking places than salons in the grand European sense. In fact, it may well be that these better speakeasies were the only grand salons, on a large scale, that the United States has ever had. There were salons, in the great days, in Boston and in Philadelphia and in Baltimore, and perhaps in Chicago, but these were confined to literary and artistic folk and the attendance at them was relatively small. The salons of the speakeasy days were numerous and they were democratic. Unlettered people and people of modest means, but who had good taste and wanted to be in superior intellectual surroundings, could go to these speakeasies and be engulfed in refined atmosphere and occasionally overhear soaring conversation, indulged in by men and women high in the arts or in the various professions. These speakeasy salons were thus gardens of general popular good taste. The Prohibition era was, in many ways, a miserable and ugly era, but it also had its more favorable aspects.

Drinks and Debate

There was a speakeasy on West Fifty-Sixth Street, between Fifth and Sixth Avenues. It was called the Napoleon. It occupied a whole building, which formerly had been the residence of an ancient and moneyed Manhattan family. The ground floor was a huge reading room, with books and magazines in sufficient numbers to have rivalled a small town library. The middle floor was the main floor. It was divided into two large rooms, a restaurant and grill, and the bar. The top floor was empty. I was there once and found only chairs and tables in disarray.

George Jean Nathan [American editor and drama critic] used to take me there occasionally. We usually went to the middle floor and stood at the bar, for a while, then took our drinks to a nearby table. The bar was built in the form of half the number eight, cut down the middle. Behind the bar were mirrors and always there were phrases written on them in soap, remarks by celebrated writers or artists. One that sticks in my mind across the years was Oscar Wilde's: "There are two great tragedies in life, one is not reaching your goal, the other is reaching it." Another was that attributed to King Gustavus Adolphus of Sweden: "Remember, my son, gold sinks in the sea, but elephant refuse floats. It is God's will." A third was the one whose authorship is problematical: "Heavenly father, give us serenity to accept what cannot be changed, courage to change what should be changed, and wisdom to know one from the other."

One evening Nathan and I were sitting alone at a table. He had just introduced me to a drink I had not had before: poussé-café, a mountainous glass with one color on top of another. The taste was somewhat sweeter than I liked, and I said so to Nathan. He smiled and said, "Wait, my boy, wait, the sweetness will soon become tart, and then bitter. Like women."

He was right. The sweetness soon became bitter.

"Angoff," he said, "that's the tragedy of women, they nearly always become bitter, sooner or later, and if they don't become bitter, they become dull. That's how women differ from men. Men improve with age, women degenerate, and they degenerate early in life. No woman can ever forgive God for giving her gray hair. Every woman is an atheist the first time she notices a gray hair in her head."

"I thought women take to the church more readily than men," I said hesitantly.

"I know, I know," said Nathan, "but that does not disprove what I have said. Women go to church but still are atheists. Women can do a thing like that. By the way, do you know who are the most atheistical women in creation?"

"Who?"

"Dancers."

"Dancers?"

"Yes, dancers," said Nathan.

He was about to continue with his philosophising when a man from an adjacent table said, "That's true. Dancers believe in nothing, not even in themselves."

The man got up and walked over to our table. He introduced himself, and the name at once registered something in my mind. I knew his name vaguely as that of an eminent choreographer. He asked us over to his table, where sat another man and two young and beautiful women. The tall man, who had come over to our table, said, "We couldn't help overhearing what you were saying about atheism and dancers, and we recognized you, Mr. Nathan. And all I want to say is that what you say is right, as far as I know dancers. The only change I would make in your statement, Mr. Nathan, is that male dancers are just as atheistical as women dancers. I have known women writers and women sculptors and women musicians, you know, and women teachers, and all of them believed in God, I don't mean they necessarily went to church, but they were believers, silent believers, non-joiners, you know; but believers. But I have never known a dancer who believed a single word in the Bible. I mean the believing parts, about the Virgin Birth, the Resurrection, and so on."

"That is the truth," said the other man, "I have seen icons in the rooms of Russian ballet dancers, and you know what they say about Russians, how they always pray and bless themselves and carry huge crucifixes, but Russian ballet dancers just look upon their icons as ornaments, like rabbits' feet or charms, ordinary charms, like dragons' teeth. They believe nothing."

The two young women merely smiled.

"What do you think?" asked Nathan of the woman with the red hair.

"I really don't know, Mr. Nathan," she said, smiling. "It never occurred to me to think about such things. I mean I don't know."

Nathan asked the other woman, the one with the black hair.

"It's hard to say," she said. "I believe in something, but what it is I can't say. Maybe it is God. Maybe it's something else."

"I have a theory," said the tall man. "Listen. Dancers, male and female, are so deeply involved with or in, whatever it is, so deeply involved in their bodies, motion, you know, are so often in the nude, almost nude, so dependent upon motion, expression through motion, that's dancing, that they simply cannot think of anything incorporeal, spiritual, God. See? People who sit believe in God, people who move around don't believe in him, or anything of that sort. I suppose, on that theory, athletes and locomotive engineers and policemen should all be atheists. But, of course, they're not. That hurts my theory, but I still think there's something in it, don't you, Mr. Nathan?"

"I like your theory," said Nathan. "I like theories that don't hold up, because theories that do hold up are surely wrong."

"For the Artistic Good of the Country"

The conversation went on far into the night, and it mounted in interest and excitement. Nathan wanted to know if dancers ever worry that their "immortality is brief." He said, "You are here today, gone tomorrow. Nijinsky can be seen no more. He can only be read about. Anna Pavlova [Vaslav Nijinsky and Anna Pavlova were Russian ballet dancers] the same. And so on."

"No," said the tall man, who appeared to be the spokesman-philosopher for the group. "We don't worry about that except when a man like you brings it up. I guess we just don't think about it. We do what we do because we like it. That's all, I guess. But what you say is probably true. We dancers are not remembered as dancers, I mean people do not see us dance after we are gone the way people read Shakespeare and Dickens and the other writers long after they're gone. But maybe that will be changed with the movies or television, if it develops to the extent that some people think it will. I don't know. In a way I hope so. In a way, I'm really not too worried. After all, what you say applies equally to actors, don't you think?"

"Oh, yes, actors, too," said Nathan, "and that's a pity."

Suddenly Nathan said, "I have a theory, too, ladies and gentlemen, and that is that all art, all the arts, are immoral. I mean that they feel hemmed in by the ordinary codes. Art essentially is anarchistic, and all artists are anarchists. No real artist believes in monogamy or in honesty or in politeness or in voting or in paying debts."

"I think that's true," said the girl with the red hair.

"I do, too," said the girl with the black hair.

"Well," said the tall man, "I don't know. Some artists are anarchists, others are not. I should say dancers are, I should say sculptors and painters are, but what about writers? I really don't know too much about them. But I seem to remember from my school days that John Bunyan was a very religious man, and I think Milton was too, wasn't he?"

"There you have me," said Nathan. "You're spoiling my theory. Perhaps my eminent colleague, Mr. Angoff, can enlighten us."

I hesitated to say anything, because I preferred to listen. But I did say something to this effect: "It's true, I'm afraid, that Milton and Bunyan were believers, in their own way, of course. Milton had his own brand of Christianity, but he believed. And I think Bunyan was a believer and Coleridge, of course. He was a minister for a while. At first he was a Unitarian, then he became a Trinitarian, or maybe it was the other way around. At least he believed, I mean, anyway he believed. But there is a great deal to Mr. Nathan's theory. Even Milton and Bunyan and Coleridge were essentially anarchistic. And I suppose it can be said that an artist, more or less instinctively, follows his own mood, wherever it may lead him, rather than the customs and beliefs of his time."

And so the discussion went on, helped along by fresh drinks. As Nathan and I walked back to his hotel, the Royalton, he said, "Maybe Prohibition is a good thing, maybe it should continue, for the artistic good of the country. Besides, I like the idea of people disobeying a foolish law.". . .

A Model of Civility

There was a speakeasy in the East Fifties. Its name escapes me, but I think it was something like The Seven Deadly Sins. It was on the ground floor. Always there was a gaudy dooropener in front; he looked like a grand admiral. The door leading into The Seven Deadly Sins was painted light blue, with two lamps on both sides. A bit in front of the door was an iron gate, decorated with iron lattice work. The grand admiral stood directly behind the gate, and opened it when a customer arrived. One of his functions was to make sure that no "strangers" or Prohibition agents tried to get in. Another was to keep sight-seers from stopping too long in front of The Seven Deadly Sins. Too much publicity was not desired by the management. It invited attention from the police and the Prohibition agents. The local police were "taken care of" [paid off], and it was to be presumed that some of the Federal agents were also "taken care of." But one couldn't always be sure that these police and agents would stay "taken care of." A new precinct captain or Federal supervisor might be appointed and he would set about doing his duty, and there could be trouble.

The Seven Deadly Sins could seat only about fifty people at most. The food was superb. It was prepared in the Viennese style. The waiters were uniformed. Young girls, dressed in Viennese fashion, were the bus-girls, and they also sold cigarettes and candy. The Seven Deadly Sins was open for lunch, but it did little in the afternoon. It did most of its business at night. The chief attraction, next to the good food and the good drinks, was the musical concert and the dancing. There was a four-piece orchestra, which played waltzes and other nostalgic European music. And always there was a singer, male or female, who joined the orchestra several times a night. There was another attraction in The Seven Deadly Sins: the huge table of snacks against the wall. There was herring and there was potato salad and there was *tort* of all sorts and there was wonderful cole slaw and there was constantly a hot pot of specially brewed coffee. One could have a full meal from this snack table alone. Indeed, some people did. There was a flat charge of $1.50 for a meal obtained this way and one could come back to the table as often as one wanted.

I was introduced to The Seven Deadly Sins by the late Stewart Holbrook [American writer], who came from the Pacific Coast. I hadn't known about it, but he had heard about it from several people in Oregon. Holbrook was a heavy drinker, well into his middle life, when he began to "take account" of himself. But he never drank when we went to The Seven Deadly Sins. I asked him why, and he answered me somewhat in this manner: "The first time I came I liked it so much here that I decided to be like these people, drink like a decent human being. But I knew I just couldn't drink moderately. One drink led to another and you know the rest. So I made a compromise. I said to myself I wouldn't drink at all here, and enjoy myself, and do my drinking outside. And not drinking here does me good, honest. I think it helps me to drink a little less outside. This is too wonderful a place for me to spoil with my drinking. You know what I like especially here?"

"What?"

"I like it because it shows me how ordinary people can live. This is the way a whole nation should be—polite, quiet, gently gay, nice music, nice dancing, good singing, good food. You know what I think?"

"What?"

"This country could be another Greece, another Rome, no, Greece is what I mean, and another Paris and Berlin and another London in the great days of these cities, spread all over the country, setting an example to everybody. The horrible thing about Hollywood is that it sets an example of living and dreaming to the United States, and that example is bad, very bad. This is a much better example for Main Street. You know, Prohibition has been a good thing in many ways, a really good thing. I don't mean the bootleg gin, the terrible joints all over the country. New York City is full of them. I mean places like this. And I'm worried."

"Worried about what?"

"That Prohibition will be repealed. Of course, Charlie, it will be. This can't go on. And I'm for repeal. But I'll be a little sorry when it happens. Places like this will vanish. The saloon will come back. Well, I'm old enough to remember the saloon. There were good ones. Good places for lonely men to come to. I mean some of them, maybe many of them. But they didn't have the class that a place like this has. You see, saloons had no orchestra music and no nice singing like here, and there were no nice, white tablecloths on the tables. A saloon is a place where you rush in and rush out, where you stand up and figure how you're gonna meet the wife and her yipping, how you're gonna meet the kids and all their yelling. It's not a home where you can spend two, three hours, being a civilized human being, where you can regain your self-respect. This place is just that. I love it."

A Poor Substitute for the Real Thing

John Arthur Henricks

During Prohibition the government added poisons to alcohol destined for industrial use to foil any would-be scofflaws and bootleggers. Much of this "denatured" alcohol was stolen or sold to bootleggers who attempted to leach out the impurities using stills. Since this was a time-consuming and expensive process, the bootleggers—lacking patience and a conscience—merely added flavors, coloring, and a lot of water to mask the bad taste. It was estimated 95 percent of all bootleg alcohol of the less reputable homemade variety contained poison. By 1927, eleven thousand people had died from drinking denatured alcohol and many more were paralyzed and/or permanently blinded.

In the following article, John Arthur Henricks, an electrochemist, discusses his Prohibition experiences with "chock beer" and "jake." The two infamous homebrews started his early career of reckless drinking that eventually put him in Alcoholics Anonymous.

It blistered my lips. It burned worse than Tabasco. It was liquid fire, the wildest, most horrible drink you can imagine. I tried some once, just to show off, in Texas where the mark of a man was not to cut your jake with water but toss it down straight. It stoned you into a weird type of intoxication, a violent, brawling, broad-chasing insanity. Matter of fact, jake got to be a police blotter nuisance. In Oklahoma respectable people rose up in arms, the church ladies screamed and the legislature finally passed a law making Jamaica ginger elixir illegal. Only the powdered gingerroot could still be used for medical purposes, but I don't think a pound of it was sold in the whole state. The bootleggers went right on supplying the same old jake. You could walk into any drugstore and with a wink get a bottle.

Another time with some Texans in Big Spring, showing off again, I was drinking lousy white corn out of a fruit jar, and I started to be derogatory about the quality of their local beverages. I told them what a civilized community we had in Chicago, where I came from, and how you could get beer, delicious beer for hot-weather drinking. "Son," said one of the Texans, "can you drink beer?" "That's my drink, boy," I said. "I was raised on beer." "Well," says he, "we reckon we can show you a little Southern hospitality and get you some beer." We drove for miles out into the brush country to a Tobacco Road character who brewed this chock beer. The name comes from the Choctaw Indians. They were kind of low-man on the Five Nations totem pole as far as bootlegging went, but they did evolve a distinctive home brew which, after yeast fermentation of malt, molasses and hops, they laced with shelled corn and raisins. I don't believe I drank more than two or three bottles. It was the damnedest stuff—practically explosive. I passed out cold.

Prohibition Encouraged Bad Habits

I became a problem drinker at about fifteen, an instant boozer. Prohibition was probably a determining factor, but by no means the only one. When the old church ladies say you're not to drink anything, it's a worthy challenge. It lighted my fuse. In high school I had as my peer group a number of buddies, all of them rebellious and openly defiant like most of the public at that time, and they drank with me. None of them became alcoholics, though, as I did.

My father drank a lot, a common thing in his line of business. He managed the Knickerbocker Ice Company in Chicago, where I was born. It was essentially a restaurant and saloon business, and he was a very gregarious type—looked like Jackie Gleason [actor best known for his television series *The Honeymooners*], hale and hearty, and he fitted right into that scene. I think the change in the quality of booze after prohibition, the horrible stuff you got, brought out the worst in him, made him a problem drinker. That and his getting older. The aging drinker loses his tolerance. My father would have qualified very well for my present fellowship. But nobody realized it then. His only admonition to me was that you should always drink like a gentleman. The old tradition. People who fell on their face were not socially acceptable.

I was still very young when my father went into a new business—freight car manufacturer and maintenance repair. It took us to New York City, where he superintended the Interboro Rapid Transit yards. We attended the Cathedral of St. John the Divine, and I was imbued with the spiritual approach, awed by the whole thing. The conflict in me between good and evil came when I was torn loose from that atmosphere—adolescence is always upsetting anyway—and transplanted to the wide open city of West Hammond, Illinois, my father's next assignment. West Hammond was so notorious that the citizenry changed the name to Calumet City, but it remained just as notorious. It vied with Cicero in ignominy.

In the church I went to there (this was well into prohibition) we had a little phenomenon common enough in churches, we had the sanctimonious closet drinker—in this instance, the choirmaster. He was a real heavy drinker, and he tried to cover it up by dousing himself with French cologne, which smelled worse to me than whiskey. We kids sneaked a drink from him now and then. There was also plenty of liquor around my house, and I dipped into that. As I say, I wasn't sixteen yet. At first it was strictly showoff, like smoking cigarettes, to impress your peers, and I made rapid headway. The DeMolay, the junior auxiliary of the Masons, a kind of Cub Scout approach to Masonry, blackballed me because of my drinking. Drinking got me into trouble at school, too. The mark of manhood in my group, as you went from knickerbockers to long pants, was to walk up one side of State Street and drink a beer in every joint—there were dozens of them—then down the other side the same way. None of us ever quite made it.

The Peak of the Bathtub Gin Era

I went to Indiana University. Those were my golden years. Hoagy Carmichael [American composer and singer] was a junior then at Indiana. He wrote some of his best music there. Bix Beiderbecke and the original Wolverines played at all our big dances. During holidays, back home in Chicago, I'd go to the Friar's Inn to drink and listen to Leon Rappolo, who invented that fantastic clarinet style whereby Benny Goodman [bandleader and clarinetist] rose to glory. . . . It was the peak of the bathtub gin era, the real white hot.

At Indiana they picked me to find some good liquor for a visitor from Wabash College, a Phi Gamma Delta man no less and a millionaire, coming to a weekend football game. This was Ed Ball, later chairman of the board of his family's Ball-Mason jar company in Muncie. We aimed to wine and dine him royally, impress him, so he'd remember us after he got to head the company. I went down to a pool hall to see my favorite bootlegger, but damned if he hadn't been knocked off in a gang shoot. So I had to pinch around and bring back what I could. It turned out to be the vilest gin ever made. I was amazed. We damn near killed Ed Ball. He laid around for hours, green and groaning. We all got deathly sick.

I couldn't graduate from Indiana because my father came down with a terminal cancer and I had to go to work. My first job was with a refinery construction company, and I traveled all over the Southwest with a bunch of wild Cal City Polack and Irish bricklayers and riveters, heavy drinkers all. We had no trouble getting a drink anywhere, not even in Oklahoma, which entered the Union as a dry state.

In Big Spring, Texas, we found a special situation. There was no budget to speak of for law enforcement officers' salaries. They had to make it themselves. The old sheriff, Jess

Robbins, and his deputies worked on a fee basis. The penalty for being drunk and disorderly was a fine of $17.80. The county got $2.80, the deputy who brought you in got $5, and Jess got $10. They only locked me up once. The reason for this immunity was because my co-workers needed somebody to bail them out, and I was in the payoff end as the materials clerk. The one time they arrested me I asked Jess, after I sobered up, how he classified offenders. "Well, you're a pretty good boy," he said. "You get your boys out, you help me. You notice I don't throw you into the cooler, though I think sometimes you've had more to drink when you come here to get them out than they had when they went in. As a general approach to the matter, if it's one of our own boys and if he can move any of his ten fingers, he really ain't drunk, but one of you damn mouthy Yankees, by God, if I can smell liquor on your breath, you're drunk and disorderly."

Oklahoma had the worst epidemic of jake foot [a limp caused by partial paralysis after drinking bad alcohol] I ever ran into. There were small towns where practically every drunk dragged one foot or the other—hundreds of cases, many of them on the way to total paralysis.

For twenty years I went on drinking practically anything alcoholic I could lay my hands on. Then in 1945 I joined AA and haven't lapsed from sobriety since.

Jake's Country Cousins

The poor man's thirst gave rise to a plethora of cheap, plentiful regional concoctions varying in potency and toxicity according to the ingredients at hand and the skill of the moonshiner. In the Deep South a relatively safe beverage was black-strap alky or pack, distilled from New Orleans molasses. The term "pack" may have derived from a British general named Packenham who died in the Battle of New Orleans in 1815 and was supposedly shipped home preserved in a cask of rum. Rugged Southwestern topers of meager means, who found the fulminating chock beer insufficiently stimulating, would add snuff to the bottles and bury them in the hot sand for further fermentation. In the

Midwest they would scoop out a hole in a block of ice, fill it with lemon extract and pour off the liquid, which, being alcohol, didn't freeze. Midwestern farmers favored pumpkin wine, prepared by emptying a pumpkin, introducing cider, alcohol or fruit, sealing the opening with wax and letting the mixture ferment for a month or so. In Kansas, another poor man's drink was white line, alcohol diluted with water; in Washington and the contiguous sections of Maryland and Virginia, panther whiskey, which had a perilously high percentage of fusel oil; in the Virginia hinterlands, jackass brandy, reputedly distilled from peaches, but likely to erode the intestines; in Philadelphia, happy Sally, jump steady, and soda pop moon, all loaded with violently toxic industrial alcohols; in Chicago, yack yack bourbon, flavored and colored with burned sugar and iodine. Skid row bums everywhere drank rub-a-dub (rubbing alcohol) and other potions containing wood alcohol, thereby courting blindness or death. Some of them would recover a few mouthfuls by squeezing Sterno through a sock.

Women and Drinking

Stanley Walker

The saloon had traditionally been a male preserve. The only women seen in bars were prostitutes and dance-hall girls. But Prohibition opened the doors for women in more ways than one. Once social drinking became fashionable, women flocked to speakeasies in droves to drink and smoke with the same zeal as their male counterparts. It was a liberating step toward the modern era. But not all bartenders and patrons enjoyed the company, relates Stanley Walker. Some speakeasy owners kept the doors closed to women just to keep the peace.

Stanley Walker was a city editor for the *New York Herald Tribune* and author of many works of nonfiction. He earned a reputation for being one of New York's most astute and resourceful newspapermen.

Soon after 1920 great, ravening hordes of women began to discover what their less respectable sisters had known for years—that it was a lot of fun, if you liked it, to get soused. All over New York these up and coming females piled out of their hideaways, rang the bells of speakeasies, wheedled drugstores into selling them gin and rye, and even in establishments of great decorum begged their escorts for a nip from a hip flask. It was all very embarrassing. Jim's corner place, although he tried to keep a reasonable amount of decorum, could not escape the howling, reeling and raging termagants. Sometimes they would merely fall down. Again they would beg for just one more drink; Jim would let them have three, watch them go to sleep and then pour

Excerpted from *The Night Club Era*, by Stanley Walker (New York: Blue Ribbon Books, Inc., 1933). Copyright © 1933 by Stanley Walker. Reprinted with permission.

them into a cab and send them home. Or one of the triangle things, husband, wife and the other woman, would decide to put on an act. There was one lady, no better, Lord knows, than she should have been, who wanted to fight when in her cups. She was rangy, and tawny-haired, and thewed like Stanley Ketchel [boxer, 1886–1910]. She could slug toe to toe with any man weighing under 200 pounds.

A New Place with New Rules

All this foolishness worried Jim. He was, for all the fact that he had once been practically a hobo, a stickler for good taste, with a little dignity thrown in if possible. When he opened the Nepenthe he announced that never, in any circumstances, would a woman ever be allowed to set foot inside the door. Many other saloon-keepers, at about this same time—that is,

---

The Legend of Hank

Bars and saloons have always been good places to spin tall tales. Even after the passage of Prohibition this oral tradition continued in speakeasies across the country. Hank the Bartender was one popular character who grew, with each retelling, to mythical proportions rivaling Paul Bunyan and Casey Jones. In the following, John Colnon relates some tall tales of Hank the Bartender to a government interviewer, J.D. Stradling, during the 1930s.

Sometimes Hank's specials were not so lucky. Joe, a bald-headed man, had been having trouble with his wife. He was feeling pretty low. "Here, try this. It'll grow hair on your chest," said Hank. It gave Joe a sudden idea. "By golly," he said, "I've tried everything else on my head, I might as well try this, too." So he took a bottle home. His wife saw him fixing to put booze on his head and knew he had been drinking again, so she beat him up and threw the bottle out the window into a crick [creek] that ran behind the house. Come Saturday, Joe went down to the crick to take a bath. Hair sprouted all over him so fast that he was shot by mistake for

men who cared more for smaller profits and less trouble than quick big money—came to the same decision. The women said that Jim was a dour old curmudgeon, a heartless woman-hater, and all that, but he kept his promise.

Not only did no woman ever come into the Nepenthe, but Jim always seemed vaguely annoyed when one called on the telephone. Now, Jim was not a woman-hater, though his private life, if any, was something which he kept carefully guarded, not more than five or six hundred persons ever suspecting anything out of the way, but he backed away from trouble. A rowdy scene in which a woman was involved would throw him into a swivet from which he wouldn't recover for days.

Thus, founded on enduring principles, backed by a man of vision and character, the Nepenthe became a sort of

---

a grizzly before he could reach his clothes.

One night Hank was mixing up something for experiment. A few drops fell on the floor. There was a mouse running around under the bar. Suddenly the mouse reared up on its hind legs, roared like a lion, and chased Hank and the bouncers right out of the place.

Not long after, a pale little man with a worried look asked Hank for a pick-me-up. Hank looked at the customer and remembered the mouse. He ran his eye over the array of bottles trying to remember what he had used. He took a little of this and a little of that with the air of an artist and the care of a drug clerk. "Try this," he said.

But Hank never made that again. The little man coughed, whooped, turned a back somersault off the stool and got up fighting mad. "Where's that cop?" he yelled and went out looking for the man on the beat. Soon the riot squad was out and when he finished up with them, the customer looked around, brushed his hands, and said: "Now where can I find them damn Marines?"

"American Life Histories: Manuscripts from the Federal Writers' Project, 1936–1940." U.S. Library of Congress Homepage, www.loc.gov.

monastery where a man, hag-ridden, beset by nightmares, tortured by the roar of far-off artillery, could retire to ponder, to smooth out the tangled web of his existence, and to conquer his soul with a firm headlock. . . .

Places like Jim's always have been havens of solace for widowers, for bitter men who were crossed in love in their youth, and for aging bachelors who would rather drink than waste their time at the annual Lonely Hearts' Ball (there was such a ball, run by Bernarr Macfadden's now dead *Graphic*). Such men are the best customers a saloon can have. Usually they are solvent and calm, and they have a quiet dignity foreign to most men who still have women folks to worry about.

No Trouble Finding Alcohol

H.L. Mencken

> H.L. Mencken was one of the most well known journalists, editors, and critics of the twenties. He was renown for being shockingly honest, sarcastic, and politically extreme. He often lampooned the Victorian way of life that governed many Americans of the time. Thus, Mencken despised Prohibition and was a loudly proclaimed "wet." He even coined a new word, "ombibulous," to describe his favor for liquor and his disfavor for Prohibition's affront to liberty. Mencken was known to often indulge his ombibulous nature by openly drinking or leading others to drink in defiance of the law. In the following essay written in the 1940s, Mencken describes these experiences, which also show how easy it was for a determined man, despite the law, to find alcohol in a Prohibition-locked America.

Prohibition went into effect on January 16, 1920, and blew up at last on December 5, 1933—an elapsed time of twelve years, ten months and nineteen days. It seemed almost a geological epoch while it was going on, and the human suffering that it entailed must have been a fair match for that of the Black Death or the Thirty Years' War, but I should say at once that my own share of the blood, sweat and tears was extremely meagre. I was, so far as I have been able to discover, the first man south of the Mason and Dixon line to brew a drinkable home-brew, and as a result my native Baltimore smelled powerfully of malt and hops during the whole horror, for I did not keep my art to myself, but imparted it to anyone who could be trusted—which meant anyone save a few abandoned Methodists, Baptists and Presbyterians, most of them already far gone in glycosuria, cholelithiasis or gastrohydrorrhea, and all of them soon so low in mind and body that they could be ignored.

Mencken's Home-Brew Academy

My seminary was run on a sort of chain-letter plan. That is to say, I took ten pupils, and then each of the ten took ten, and so on *ad infinitum*. There were dull dogs in Baltimore who went through the course forty or fifty times, under as many different holders of my degrees, and even then never got beyond a nauseous *Malzsuppe* [wort which is the malt mixture base for making beer], fit only for policemen and Sunday-school superintendents. But there were others of a much more shining talent, and I put in a great deal of my time in 1921 and 1922 visiting their laboratories, to pass judgment on their brews. They received me with all the deference due to a master, and I was greatly bucked up by their attentions. In fact, those attentions probably saved me from melancholia, for during the whole of the twelve years, ten months and nineteen days I was a magazine editor, and a magazine editor is a man who lives on a sort of spiritual Bataan [besieged island] with bombs of odium taking him incessantly from the front and torpedoes of obloquy [disrepute] harrying him astern.

But I would not have you think that I was anything like dependent, in that abominable time, upon home-brew, or that I got down any really formidable amount of it. To be sure, I had to apply my critical powers to many thousands of specimens, but I always took them in small doses, and was careful to blow away a good deal of the substance with the foam. This home-brew, when drinkable at all, was a striking proof of the indomitable spirit of man, but in the average case it was not much more. Whenever the mood to drink purely voluptuously was on me I preferred, of course, the product of professional brewmasters, and, having been born lucky, I usually found it. Its provenance, in those days, was kept a kind of military secret, but now that the nightmare is over and jails no longer yawn I do not hesitate to say that, in so far as my own supply went, most of it came from the two lowermost tiers of Pennsylvania counties. Dotted over that smiling pastoral landscape there were groups of small breweries that managed successfully, by means that we need not go into, to stall off the prohibition agents, and I had the privilege and honor of getting down many a carboy [large glass bottles used for fermenting beer] of their excellent product both in Baltimore, where I lived, and in New York, where I had my office.

When I say New York I mean the city in its largest sense—the whole metropolitan region. As a matter of fact, the malt liquor on tap on the actual island of Manhattan was usually bad, and often downright poisonous. When I yearned for a quaff of the real stuff I went to Union Hill, N.J., and if not to Union Hill, then to Hoboken. Both of these great outposts radiated a bouquet of malt and hops almost as pungent as Baltimore's, and in Union Hill there was a beer-house that sticks in my memory as the most comfortable I have ever encountered on this earth. Its beers were perfect, its victuals were cheap and nourishing, its chairs were designed by osteological engineers specializing in the structure of the human pelvis, and its waiters, Axel, Otto, Julius and Raymond, were experts at their science. This incomparable dump was discovered by the late Philip Goodman, then transiently a theatrical manager on Broadway and all his life a fervent beer-drinker, and he and I visited it every time I was in New York, which was pretty often. We would ease into our canons' stalls in the early evening and continue in residence until Axel, Otto, Julius and Raymond began to snore in their corner and the colored maintenance engineer, Willie, turned his fire-hose into the washroom. Then back by taxi to Weehawken [township in northeastern New Jersey], from Weehawken to Forty-second street by the six-minute ferry, and from Forty-second street by taxi again to the quick, lordly sleep of quiet minds and pure hearts.

A Road Trip to Elysium

The fact that the brews on tap in that Elysium [mythical Greek paradise where heroes were sent] came from lower Pennsylvania naturally suggested an expedition to the place of their origin, and Goodman and I laid many plans for making the trip in his car. But every time we started out we dropped in on Axel, Otto, Julius and Raymond for stirrup cups [drinking vessel associated with hunting and in the shape of an animal], and that was as far as we ever got. Alone, however, I once visited Harrisburg on newspaper business, and there had the felicity of drinking close to the *Urquell* [source]. That was in the primitive days when New York still bristled with peepholes and it was impossible to get into a strange place without a letter from a judge, but in Harrisburg there were no formalities. I simply approached a traffic cop and asked him where reliable stuff was to be had. "Do you see that kaif [café] there?" he replied, pointing to the corner. "Well, just go in and lay down your money. If you don't like it, come back and I'll give you another one." I liked it well enough, and so did not trouble him further.

It's Who You Know

I should add, however, that I once came so near going dry in Pennsylvania, and in the very midst of a huge fleet of illicit breweries, that the memory of it still makes me shiver. This was at Bethlehem in the Lehigh Valley, in 1924. I had gone to the place with my publisher, Alfred Knopf, to hear the celebrated Bach Choir, and we were astounded after the first day's sessions to discover that not a drop of malt liquor was to be had in the local pubs. This seemed strange and unfriendly, for it is well known to every musicologist that the divine music of old Johann Sebastian cannot be digested without the aid of its natural solvent. But so far as we could make out there was absolutely none on tap in the Lehigh Valley, though we searched high and low, and threw ourselves upon the mercy of cops, taxi-drivers, hotel clerks, the Elks, the rev. clergy, and half the tenors and basses of the choir. All reported that prohibition agents had been sighted in the mountains a few days before, and that as a result hundreds of kegs had been buried and every bartender was on the alert. How we got through the second day's sessions I don't know; the music was magnificent, but our tonsils became so parched that we could barely join in the final Amen. Half an hour before our train was scheduled to leave for New York we decided to go down to the Lehigh station and telegraph to a bootician in the big city, desiring him to start westward at once and meet us at Paterson, N.J. On the way

A federal agent smashes a barrel of bootleg whiskey. Despite the efforts of law enforcement, alcohol was easy to obtain during Prohibition.

to the station we discussed this madcap scheme dismally, and the taxi-driver overheard us. He was a compassionate man, and his heart bled for us.

"Gents," he said, "I hate to horn in on what ain't none of my business, but if you feel that bad about it I think I know where some stuff is to be had. The point is, can you get it?"

We at once offered him money to introduce us, but he waved us off.

"It wouldn't do you no good," he said. "These Pennsylvania Dutch never trust a hackman."

"But where is the place?" we breathed.

"I'm taking you to it," he replied, and in a moment we were there.

It was a huge, blank building that looked like a forsaken warehouse, but over a door that appeared to be tightly locked there was the telltale sign, "Sea Food"—the universal euphemism for beerhouse in Maryland and Pennsylvania throughout the thirteen awful years. We rapped on the door and presently it opened about half an inch, revealing an eye and part of a mouth. The ensuing dialogue was *sotto voce* [in soft terms] but *staccato* [abrupt and disconnected sounds] and *appassionata* [impassioned]. The eye saw that we were famished, but the mouth hesitated.

"How do I know," it asked, "that you ain't two of them agents?"

The insinuation made us boil, but we had to be polite.

"*Agents!*" hissed Knopf. "What an idea! Can't you *see* us? Take a good look at us."

The eye looked, but the mouth made no reply.

"Can't you tell musicians when you see them?" I broke in. "Where did you ever see a prohibition agent who looked so innocent, so moony, so dumb? We are actually fanatics. We came here to hear Bach. Is this the way Bethlehem treats its guests? We came a thousand miles, and now—"

"*Three* thousand miles," corrected Knopf.

"*Five* thousand," I added, making it round numbers.

Suddenly I bethought me that the piano score of the B minor mass had been under my arm all the while. What better introduction? What more persuasive proof of our *bona fides?* I held up the score and pointed to the title on the cover. The eye read:

J.S. Bach

Mass in B Minor

The eye flicked for an instant or two, and then the mouth spoke. "Come in, gents," it said. As the door opened our natural momentum carried us into the bar in one leap, and there we were presently immersed in two immense *Humpen* [a large cylindrical vessel made in Germany]. The quality we did not pause to observe; what we mainly recalled later was the astounding modesty of the bill, which was sixty-five cents for five *Humpen*—Knopf had two and I had three—and two sandwiches. We made our train just as it was pulling out.

Another Crisis

It was a narrow escape from death in the desert, and we do not forget all these years afterward that we owed it to Johann Sebastian Bach, that highly talented and entirely respectable man, and especially to his mass in B minor. In the great city of Cleveland, Ohio, a few months later, I had much worse luck. I went there, in my capacity of newspaper reporter, to help cover the Republican national convention which nominated Calvin Coolidge [soon to become the 30th president of the United States 1923–1929] and I assumed like everyone else that the prohibition agents would lay off while the job was put through, if only as a mark of respect to their commander-in-chief. This assumption turned out to be erroneous. The agents actually clamped down on Cleveland with the utmost ferocity, and produced a drought that was virtually complete. Even the local cops and newspaper reporters were dry, and many of the latter spent a large part of their time touring the quarters of the out-of-town correspondents, begging for succor. But the supplies brought in by the correspondents were gone in a few days, and by the time the convention actually opened a glass of malt liquor was as hard to come by in Cleveland as an honest politician.

Bootlegging Misadventure

The news of this horror quickly got about, and one morning I received a dispatch in cipher from a Christian friend in Detroit, saying that he was loading a motor-launch with ten cases of bottled beer and ale, and sending it down the Detroit river and across Lake Erie in charge of two of his goons. They were instructed, he said, to notify me the instant they arrived off the Cleveland breakwater. Their notice reached me the next afternoon, but by that time the boys were nominating Cal, so I could not keep the rendezvous myself, but had to send an agent. This agent was Paul de Kruif, then a young man of thirty-four, studying the literary art under my counsel. Paul was a fellow of high principles and worthy of every confidence; moreover, he was dying of thirst himself. I started him out in a rowboat, and he was gone three hours. When he got back he was pale and trembling, and I could see at a glance that some calamity had befallen. When he got his breath he gasped out the story.

The two goons, it appeared, had broken into their cargo on the way down from Detroit, for the weather was extremely hot. By the time they anchored off the Cleveland breakwater they had got down three cases, and while they were waiting for de Kruif they knocked off two more. This left but five—and they figured that it was just enough to get them back to Detroit, for the way was uphill all the way, as a glance at a map will show. De Kruif, who was a huge and sturdy Dutchman with a neck like John L. Sullivan [a world heavyweight bare-knuckle boxing champion 1882–1892], protested violently and even undertook to throw them overboard and pirate the launch and cargo, but they pulled firearms on him, and the best he could do was to get six bottles. These he drank on his return in the rowboat, for the heat, as I have said, was extreme. As a result, I got nothing whatsoever; indeed, not a drop of malt touched my throat until the next night at 11:57, when the express for Washington and points East crossed the frontier of the Maryland Free State.

This was my worst adventure during prohibition, and in many ways it remains the worst adventure of my whole life.

Chapter 5

Repeal

Chapter Preface

The "wet" forces did not give up the Prohibition debate after the passage of the Eighteenth Amendment. They immediately set their sights on repealing Prohibition, despite the difficulty that would be involved. Repealing a constitutional amendment required two-thirds congressional support, a feat that had never been achieved in U.S. history. The votes of only thirteen states in the nation could block the measure. That was considerably less support than was required to pass the Eighteenth Amendment. The prospect was so daunting, in fact, that "dry" forces let their guard down. Prohibition advocates were overconfident in the power of the law that repeal appeared impossible.

As Prohibition wore on crime and corruption increased. Even die-hard prohibitionists like evangelist Billy Sunday saw that the laws were causing more problems than they were solving. Some prohibitionists advocated modifying the law, but this effort split dry forces, many of whom stubbornly supported leaving the law unchanged. By 1930 even conservative candidates were supporting repeal. President Herbert Hoover, however, remained an exception. Despite the advice of the Republican Party, Hoover clung to his support of Prohibition during his bid for reelection. Conversely, the Democratic Party, led by presidential candidate Franklin Roosevelt, officially called for an end to Prohibition.

Prohibition was repealed in February 1933. Congress approved the Twenty-first Amendment, which repealed the Eighteenth. By December it would be ratified by three-fourths of the states. Newly elected president Franklin Roosevelt signed the proclamation at 7:00 P.M. on December 5. The results were almost immediately perceptible. Millions of dollars in liquor tax filled federal coffers, and many new jobs in the liquor industry were created at a time the country needed them the most. Roosevelt further declared that the liquor tax would be kept low enough to make bootlegging unprofitable. Crime and corruption did decrease though it would not disappear. Criminals merely moved into other illegal pursuits. But the relationships criminals established during Prohibition were kept long after the Eighteenth Amendment had been retired.

A United Cause

Grace C. Root

No organization put more effort into defeating Prohibition than the Women's Organization for National Prohibition Reform (WONPR). Founded by the wife of Charles Sabine, an influential businessman, the WONPR evolved into a powerful political organization with a million members and chapters in forty-four states. The WONPR became the political antithesis of the Woman's Christian Temperance Union.

The WONPR did not advocate the return of the old saloon and its rowdy lawlessness but did believe Prohibition was a failure. The following selection is the WONPR's Declaration of Principles. It lists their mission statement and the reasons why Prohibition should be repealed. The declaration details the organization's belief that the government did not have any right to force temperance onto the people. The selection also mentions the disastrous consequences of Prohibition including loss of life, property, and individual rights.

DECLARATION OF PRINCIPLES

1. We are convinced that National Prohibition is fundamentally wrong,

(a) Because it conflicts with the basic American principle of local home rule and destroys the balance, established by the framers of our government, between powers delegated to the Federal authority and those reserved to the sovereign states or to the people themselves,

(b) And because its attempt to impose total abstinence by national governmental fiat ignores the truth that no law will be respected or can be enforced unless supported by the moral sense and the common conscience of the communities affected by it.

2. We are convinced that National Prohibition, wrong in principle, has been equally disastrous in consequences in the hypocrisy, the corruption, the tragic loss of life and the appalling increase of crime which have attended the abortive attempt to enforce it; in the checking of the steady growth of temperance which had preceded it; in the shocking effect it has had upon the youth of the nation; in the impairment of constitutional guarantees of individual rights; in the weakening of the sense of solidarity between the citizen and the government which is the only sure basis of a country's strength.

The Women's Organization for National Prohibition Reform records these convictions and declares:

That eleven years' experience of National Prohibition has demonstrated its adoption to have been a grievous mistake, persistence in which will constitute a continuing threat to our country's well being.

That in the removal from the Federal Constitution of a provision which should never have been put into it lies the only reasonable hope of relief from conditions which have become intolerable.

That in our judgment a repeal adopted by the people of the requisite number of states and the restoration to each state of its former power to regulate the manufacture, sale and transportation of intoxicating beverages within its own limits should be accompanied by adequate state regulatory enactments forbidding the return of the saloon and responsive to the sentiments of the people and therefore capable of enforcement.

That such enactments would drive the crime-breeding speakeasies of the present day to the same extinction that has already met the saloon as an institution of our national life.

That the Federal government, exercising its power to regulate interstate and foreign commerce should protect each state in the enforcement of its state laws according to its true function.

That the people of the United States who have never had the opportunity to pass judgment upon this question should be given such an opportunity and that therefore, that this may be accomplished in an orderly way and in accord with Constitutional procedure, we urge the Congress to submit to conventions of the people in the several states rather than to the legislatures thereof, a resolution for the repeal of the Eighteenth Amendment.

An Unfair, Unenforceable, and Un-American Law

Ira L. Reeves

> Ira L. Reeves was a hard-line, teetotaling army colonel appointed to be the Prohibition administrator in the very "wet" state of New Jersey. He plunged into the job with the intent to dry out the district. The first thing he did was remove corrupt officials. Then he went straight for the source of the problem by raiding underground breweries and stills, as opposed to speakeasies. But Reeves found the public as well as local police agencies to be uncooperative and even hostile to his tactics. Some of his agents were even arrested by local police for firing their guns into the air when an angry mob threatened them. A frustrated Reeves resigned from his post four months later.
>
> The following chapter is from his book *Ol' Rum River* in which Reeves advocates the total repeal of the Eighteenth Amendment. In it, he details why Prohibition is impossible to enforce and cites examples from his own experiences. He also explains why Prohibition in its current form encourages lawlessness and tramples the notion of personal liberty.

S hould the Eighteenth Amendment be repealed? I shall base the argument on my observations and experiences as a prohibition administrator and on my subsequent investigations.

The Eighteenth Amendment is out of harmony with every other clause, sentence, paragraph, Section and Article of, and Amendment to, the Constitution of the United States. It deprives the citizens of guaranteed rights under other provisions of the Constitution and usurps police functions properly belonging to the separate states.

It is wholly out of harmony with the American ideals of liberty as fought for by our forefathers and reverts back to the conception of the supremacy of the State existing two or more centuries ago.

It has never been enforced in any measurable degree of effectiveness from the date of its adoption to the present day, and it will not, and cannot, be enforced. The resultant immunity enjoyed by its violators has bred disrespect for all laws.

It has robbed the Federal Government and the States of revenues rightfully due them and placed more than the equivalent of such revenues in the hands of bootleggers, gangsters, racketeers, and other criminals who have utilized the resultant wealth to purchase immunity against all law. The corrupt use of these ill-gotten gains is largely responsible for the present reign of crime and the corruption of thousands of public officials.

It's Made the Problem Worse

The Eighteenth Amendment has increased rather than decreased the use of alcoholic beverages. It has increased the price and the quantity, and lowered the quality, much of the present liquor being poisoned, as a result of the Government's own acts, and thus directly responsible for thousands of cases of blindness, paralysis, "jake" [jake-walk, the shuffle that resulted from partial paralysis], and death.

The Eighteenth Amendment sets up a super-religion and the false doctrine of control of morals by law confuses prohibition with temperance, and attempts to make the two words synonymous.

It has been my good fortune to visit many states in the Union and practically all the larger cities since prohibition was adopted, and to make first-hand observations of conditions as they exist under the operation of the Eighteenth Amendment and its twin offspring, the Volstead Act and the Jones Law [the Jones Law increased sentences for violators of the Volstead Act]. The author of the former is no longer in Congress and the latter now disclaims responsibility for his namesake. "It's a wise child that knows its own father," and it now seems that the Jones Law is not a wise child. One law is an orphan and the other of doubtful paternity. The mother, of course, is in both cases the Anti-Saloon League.

In support of my first contention, namely, that the Eighteenth Amendment is out of harmony with every other clause, sentence, paragraph, Section and Article of, and Amendment to, the Constitution of the United States, deprives the citizens of guaranteed rights under other provisions of the Constitution, and usurps police functions properly belonging to the separate States, I submit that the first nine amendments to the Constitution of the United States were adopted shortly after the Constitution itself became effective. They are commonly known as the "Bill of Rights." In each and every one of them the State recognizes rights and privileges properly belonging to the citizen. Therefore, it was a perfectly proper procedure that the adoption of those amendments was referred to the legislatures of the several States rather than to conventions of the people.

On the other hand, the Eighteenth Amendment *takes something away* from the citizens and the States. It recognizes no rights or privileges but restricts them instead. By referring this Amendment to the State Legislatures, it may have been legally adopted but it certainly was not morally adopted. You can concede or recognize the rights of people without asking their consent, but you have no moral right to take anything away from them which is prized by them, without their consent.

One Amendment Violates the Rest

Friends of prohibition accuse us, who disagree with them, of having no respect for the Constitution because we dare to challenge the good faith and consistency of one amendment only, and because we charge that Amendment with being contradictory to the first nine amendments and the spirit of every other section and article of the principal document. I want, in turn, to challenge the challengers and question their respect for the Constitution when they sponsored this iniquitous ordinance, which is in no sense a basic law, and secured its adoption by less than five thousand uninstructed state legislators—not giving the millions of other citizens an opportunity to vote on it.

At no time in the history of our country has the Government in Washington assumed such intimate police powers over the individual citizens of the several States as it has in the attempted enforcement of this prohibition amendment. Such an assumption of authority is so absolutely out of harmony with our conception of government, with our understanding as to the functions of the central Government, that the revolt against it by the citizens, and by the State, municipal, and county law enforcement agencies, is but an outward expression of their inward contempt for it.

When I was a Federal prohibition administrator I made every effort to cooperate, offered every concession and every inducement to the local police and sheriffs to aid me in my work, but my efforts were no more successful in securing cooperation than one would have if one tried to get teamwork between a bulldog and a tomcat in chasing a rabbit.

As for me, I have more confidence in my neighbors—even the overadvertised police—than I have in any Federal prohibition group I ever saw. If we cannot trust our neighbors in our cities, in our counties, in our States, to enforce a law, then there can be no hope of its enforcement.

As an argument to cajole the States to assist in enforcing this un-American law, its friends try to make you believe that before National Prohibition was adopted, many States already had prohibition. They try to mislead by the clever use of words. Let me state right here, and I challenge anyone to refute it, that no State in the Union had the equivalent of the Eighteenth Amendment with its Volstead Act and Jones Law and Prohibition Unit, at any time prior to the adoption of the Eighteenth Amendment. Michigan had the nearest approach to it—but look at Michigan today. . . .

Taking a Step Backward

Let me state my second contention: The Eighteenth Amendment is wholly out of harmony with the American ideals of liberty as fought for by our forefathers and reverts back to the conception of the supremacy of the State existing two or more centuries ago.

In the early days of the American colonies, the sturdy pioneers believed, as their ancestors had believed for centuries, that the State was a thing separate and apart from the people and that its authority over its subjects was second only to God. This conception changed before the middle of the eighteenth century. A new conception of the sovereignty of the people and the reserved rights of the individual became the ideal. This new idea found expression in the Declaration of Independence, which has given, not only to us but to all the rest of mankind, a definition of liberty.

The Eighteenth Amendment has attempted to efface the Preamble to the Declaration of Independence and of the Bill of Rights as expressed in the early amendments to the Constitution, and would return to us the old conception of the power of the State as being supreme, regardless of what human liberties may be trampled under foot. It is the return to the conception of an absolute monarchy, or of a tyrant. It is generous to say that it is Neroic. . . .

Prohibition Cannot Be Enforced

My third contention is: The Eighteenth Amendment has never been enforced in any measurable degree of effectiveness from the date of its adoption to the present day and will not and cannot be enforced. The immunity thus enjoyed by its violators has bred disrespect for all law.

Any criminal law, to be enforceable, must have a preponderance of public sentiment behind it. Prohibition has no such preponderance; and what sentiment there is remaining, is rapidly fading away.

There is not another municipal, State or National law, statute, or ordinance in the United States, which in any way involves criminality, which has not at least ninety-nine percent of the sentiment of good citizens behind it, and yet many of these criminal laws are poorly enforced. How then can one expect any large measure of enforcement of the Eighteenth Amendment and the laws thereunder when, to be generous, we will concede a few besides the paid professional reformers to be militantly for them, less than thirty percent passively in favor of them, and the remainder of our citizens who are against them, ranging all the way from passive resistance to open rebellion? . . .

Three Possible Futures

The Eighteenth Amendment has one of three possible futures and we can take our choice. It will either be repealed, liberally modified, or, through popular nullification, become as dead as a smoked herring.

Even harmonious cooperation between both State and Federal Government enforcement agencies would be unable to secure any measure of success. But Federal agencies and State officers have never worked together harmoniously in the accomplishment of a common end. In the matter of prohibition enforcement this psychological situation is most evident. We will never have full State cooperation or municipal police cooperation as long as the Federal Government takes the major part in this attempted enforcement—as long as prohibition is primarily a Federal function. We will have to choose between the two: either our own sheriffs, our own police and constables, with whom we are in daily contact and whom by our vote we have placed in authority, must assume the task of enforcing regulations of the State; or if it is a Federal function, such enforcement must be left to the carpet-bagger Federal agent who has no interest in us or our community and in most instances is more concerned with what he can get out of the law than with what he can put into it.

As paradoxical and unmoral as it may seem, the greatest

measure of Federal success under the present national prohibition law is the artistic work of the trained "shake-down" prohibition agent. In his curbstone court he will "shake down" the offender for, say, $100 to $500; while more frequently than not, were the offender arrested, the courts would grant a continuance, or impose a small fine or short jail sentence, except on "bargain day." Imagine it—a "bargain day"—the great Federal courts of the United States of America offering bargains to criminals under the Volstead Act. On "bargain day" the offender might frequently get off with a nominal fine, if he should plead guilty, and thus show that the great power of the United States had been triumphantly vindicated.

More bootleggers are put out of business through the Federal and State "shake-down" system than through conviction by the Federal and State courts!

Doff your hats, ye "sacred law" Dodos, and stand at respectful attention while the gangsters, the grafters, the Anti-Saloon League proudly goose-step by in reverential review!

If one will carefully analyze the merits, real or alleged of prohibition, one will find that its enforcement is involved in a maze of IFS. This might well be termed the IF Amendment to the Constitution. Some of the sub-headings of the IF Amendment are:

If prohibition can be enforced.

If we can get honest men to enforce it.

If such men will remain honest.

If local police and State authorities will cooperate with Federal agencies in enforcing the law.

If people will not patronize the bootleggers.

If people will assist the authorities by tattling against their neighbors.

If it can be made a moral issue and not a political one.

If thousands of church members will stop being hypocrites—"dry-ocrits," voting dry and drinking wet.

If all these *ifs* can be realized, or *if* a few of them can be vitalized, there might be some measure of hope; but I do not know how that end is to be accomplished, and I do not believe anyone else can offer a solution to the problem of this multiplicity of *ifs*. When a prohibition administrator, I tried to overcome most of them, but I soon found that my task was one of reforming human nature and not one of enforcing the law. . . .

If, with all this concentration of strength and legal talent, snoopers, snipers, and all the rest, no measure of decent enforcement is possible, what are you going to do with the remainder of the United States?

Already more people have been killed in the battle of enforcement and in the wars over disputed bootlegging territory, than were killed on the field of battle on the side of the patriots in our War for Independence. And the battle has just begun. Where and when will it end, and who will count the casualties?

I believe that all reasonable prohibitionists admit that the law so far has been a failure. The most recent argument seems to be a plea to give it more time. Why give it more time? Give a cancer more time and it will eat out your face until your features are no longer recognizable. Cut it out while its roots are sufficiently short to be reached with a knife and do not allow them to worm their way, snake-like, into every fiber of our national being, ultimately to destroy us as a nation.

The Money Goes Outside the System

My fourth contention is: The Eighteenth Amendment has robbed the Federal Government and the States of revenues rightfully due them and placed more than the equivalent of such revenues in the hands of bootleggers, gangsters, racketeers, and other criminals, who have utilized the resultant wealth to purchase immunity against all law. The corrupt use of these ill-gotten gains is largely responsible for the present reign of crime and the corruption of thousands of public officials. . . .

A factor in connection with enforcement of the prohibition laws which is seldom if ever considered is that graft money for the most part does not pass through the hands of the receiving tellers of banks, but goes into safety deposit boxes. It is also true that many bootleggers in order to cover up their activities also deposit their ill-gotten gains in safety deposit boxes. With the vast amount of money passing through the hands of the bootleggers and grafting officials it can be readily seen that the amount of cash removed from circulation through these grafting activities runs into many millions of dollars.

Alcoholism Has Actually Increased

In my fifth contention I said: The Eighteenth Amendment has increased rather than decreased the use of alcoholic beverages. It has increased the price and quantity, and lowered the quality, much of the present liquor being poisoned as a result of the Government's own acts, and thus directly responsible for thousands of cases of blindness, paralysis, "jake," and death.

The Prohibitionists contend that there is less drinking in the United States today than there was before prohibition. This statement, of course, cannot be proven. We certainly cannot depend on statistics, for reliable statistics are not available. We have, of course, statistics as to the number of gallons consumed before prohibition, but there is no way on earth of determining the amount consumed at the present time, because at least 95 percent of it is home-made, or comes from moonshine stills, and "wildcat" breweries. One can search all the bureaus in Washington and one will not find a single "wildcat" still which has reported the number of gallons it manufactures. Neither do the home stills and home brewers report, nor do the "wildcat" brewers located in barns, chicken-houses, pigeon cotes, and a thousand other camouflaged locations.

I had a part in raids leading to the capture of several hundred stills, breweries, ale plants, "cutting plants" and other producers of liquor. The amount of liquor actually on hand at the time of capture ran into hundreds of thousands of gallons. It was rarely found that the liquor on hand represented more than a week's run—usually less. Some of these stills had evidence of having been active for months. They did not make the stuff unless it was readily sold, and when sold, it was, of course, sold for consumption.

The Government has no possible means of knowing, or even roughly estimating, the amount of liquor turned by these plants. Naturally, there are no reports. . . .

Confusing Prohibition with Temperance

Let me restate my sixth contention: The Eighteenth Amendment sets up a super-religion, and the false doctrine of control of morals by law confuses prohibition with true temperance and attempts to make the two words synonymous.

Prohibitionists contend that the Eighteenth Amendment and the laws thereunder are moral, not political, issues. If they are moral issues, how in "Kingdom Come" do we expect to enforce them with a body of men, but comparatively few of whom have any idea of temperance or respect for the law they are trying to enforce? If they are moral issues, why is it that the very organization trying to make us more moral with a shotgun has proved to be a training school for bootleggers? Show me one ex-prohibition agent who is leading a decent life since leaving the service, and I will show you two who are engaged in bootlegging, rum-running, guarding gangsters, or some other activity allied with the bootlegging industry.

I use the word "industry" advisedly, for bootlegging is among the principal industries, if not *the* leading industry of the United States today.

Friends of prohibition say the answer to this situation is to "get honest men to enforce the prohibition laws."

They fail to say how this may be done. . . .

Temperance is a moral issue. Temperance puts up to the individual the right to choose and decide and in so doing, to develop character, stability, individuality. It recognizes the biblical principle that man is a free moral agent.

Prohibition is strictly a political issue—a political football—and will always remain so. It places the power of the States above that of individual decision. The doctrine of prohibition, if carried to its ultimate conclusion, would make us a nation of mollycoddles. It would destroy the power of individual resistance. The more we lean on extraneous support, the fewer props we have within us to support our character.

It is divine law that nothing of value in this world develops without resistance. But according to the prohibition idea, if we want strength of character we must get Uncle Sam to throw his protecting army of shotgun artists, snoopers, grafters, and busybodies around our homes and tell us "Thou Shalt Not."

Many proponents of prohibition claim justification on grounds of morality and high principle, when in truth prohibition is wholly unjustifiable because it violates a basic principle of Christian ethics—viz: *The end does not justify the means.* . . .

History teaches that every attempt at a democratic form of government which has failed has been wrecked on the rock of overcentralization of governmental functions. Prohibition is the most revolutionary step toward centralization of authority we have ever taken since our Constitution was first adopted. Let Americans take warning and observe the lessons of history. No time should be lost in returning to the citizens and to the States the rights that the Eighteenth Amendment took away from them. End the drift toward centralization of governmental powers—repeal the Amendment—let the people rule again.

A Dry Admits Prohibition's Failure

John D. Rockefeller Jr.

> By 1932 much of the nation was eager to see Prohibition
> ended. Repeal rallies and marches filled the streets of major
> cities. Democratic and Republican political nominees scram-
> bled to endorse a pro-"wet" platform. Even the most diehard
> prohibitionist could see that repeal was a serious threat, if not
> an inevitability. Industrialist John D. Rockefeller Jr. was an
> admitted teetotaler and one of the most dedicated prohibition-
> ists. He had donated more than $350,000 to the Anti-Saloon
> League over the years. He, like many of his colleagues,
> believed Prohibition would increase worker productivity. But
> Prohibition had actually created more problems among work-
> ers as well as fostering in them a disrespect for the law. The
> onset of the Great Depression added greatly to these prob-
> lems. Rockefeller could no longer ignore the reality of Prohi-
> bition's failure and made a painful decision. He wrote the fol-
> lowing open letter to the president of Columbia University
> announcing his official support for repeal of the Eighteenth
> Amendment. It struck a mortal blow to the "dry" cause.

My position may surprise you, as it will many of my
friends. I was born a teetotaler [one who doesn't
drink]; all my life I have been a teetotaler on principle. Neither my father nor his father ever tasted a drop of intoxicating liquor, nor have I. My mother and her mother were
among the dauntless women of their day, who, hating the

From "Text of Rockefeller's Letter to Dr. Butler," by John D. Rockefeller Jr., *New York
Times*, June 7, 1932.

horrors of drunkenness, were often found with bands of women of like mind, praying on their knees in the saloons in their ardent desire to save men from the evils that so commonly sprang from those sources of iniquity. Although a teetotaler on principle and in practice, I have always stood for whatever measure seemed at the time to give promise of best promoting temperance. With my father, I for years supported the Anti-Saloon League in both its State and national work. It was at one time reported that our contributions toward the passage of the Eighteenth Amendment amounted to between $15,000,000 and $30,000,000. As I have previously stated, from the year 1900 up to and including the date of passage of the Eighteenth Amendment, the contributions of my father and myself to all branches of the Anti-Saloon League, Federal and State—the only contributions made by us in support of prohibition legislation aggregated $350,000.

Unabashed Disregard for the Law

When the Eighteenth Amendment was passed I earnestly hoped—with a host of advocates of temperance—that it would be generally supported by public opinion and thus the day be hastened when the value to society of men with minds and bodies free from the undermining effects of alcohol would be generally realized. That this has not been the result, but rather that drinking generally has increased; that the speakeasy has replaced the saloon, not only unit for unit, but probably two-fold if not three-fold; that a vast army of lawbreakers has been recruited and financed on a colossal scale; that many of our best citizens, piqued at what they regarded as an infringement of their private rights, have openly and unabashed disregarded the Eighteenth Amendment; that as an inevitable result respect for all law has been greatly lessened; that crime has increased to an unprecedented degree—I have slowly and reluctantly come to believe.

I am not unmindful of the great blessing which the abolition of the saloon has been to our country or of certain other benefits that have resulted from the adoption of the

Eighteenth Amendment. It is my profound conviction, however, that these benefits, important and far reaching as they are, are more than outweighed by the evils that have developed and flourished since its adoption, evils which, unless promptly checked, are likely to lead to conditions unspeakably worse than those which prevailed before.

A First Step to Restore the Nation

It is not to be expected that the repeal of the Eighteenth Amendment will in itself end all these evils and restore public respect for law. I believe, however, that its repeal is a prerequisite to the attainment of that goal. I am informed that should repeal become effective, all the machinery for controlling the liquor traffic built up in the respective States and in the nation throughout the many years prior to the enactment of the Eighteenth Amendment would with few exceptions be in force, strengthened by various Federal laws and court decisions having to do with the regulation of interstate commerce. Moreover, were the Eighteenth Amendment to be repealed, sufficient time ought to be given before repeal became effective to permit the various States through legislative action representing public opinion to set up such new safeguards or methods with reference to the handling of alcoholic beverages as seemed best calculated to ensure adequate and proper control of the traffic in the interest of temperance, and at the same time safeguard the normal liberty of action of the individual.

There are many who, feeling as I do that the Eighteenth Amendment has not accomplished the object which its enactment sought to attain, would willingly favor its repeal were some alternate method that gave promise of better results offered as a substitute. In my judgment it will be so difficult for our people as a whole to agree in advance on what the substitute should be, and so unlikely that any one method will fit the entire nation, that repeal will be far less possible if coupled with an alternate measure. For that reason I the more strongly approve the simple, clear-cut position you are proposing to recommend and which I shall count it not only a duty but a privilege to support.

My hope is that the tremendous effort put forth in behalf of the Eighteenth Amendment by millions of earnest, consecrated people will be continued in effective support of practical measures for the promotion of genuine temperance. To that cause my own efforts will ever be devoted.

A Vote for Repeal

Franklin D. Roosevelt

In the following speech made in 1932, presidential candidate
Franklin D. Roosevelt made it clear that a vote for him and
his party was a vote for repeal. He accuses the Republicans of
being vague about the repeal issue, which is ironic. Former
New York governor, Al Smith had accused Roosevelt of the
same thing years earlier. Roosevelt supported repeal but
remained silent about the issue so as not to inflame the drys.
Al Smith had to goad Roosevelt into coming out and making
repeal a major issue on the Democratic plank.

Roosevelt wasted no time in making the issue his own.
After he was elected president, he quickly fulfilled his campaign promise to end Prohibition. The Eighteenth Amendment was voided in three days and the measure ratified within
the year. By December 5, 1933, hard liquor was legalized.

M y friends:
Once upon a time an orator who was describing the
scenery of his State remarked that in the North it was
"mountaineous" and that in the South it was "moisterious."

That classic description reminds me of the Republican national ticket this year—"high and dry" at one end and at the
other end "increasing moisture."

But before I come to further elucidation on that point let
me make another clear.

However we may differ as to method, we all agree that
temperance is one of the cardinal virtues. In dealing with the
great social problems in my own State, such as the care of

Excerpted from *The Public Addresses of Franklin D. Roosevelt*, by Franklin D. Roosevelt
(New York: Random House, 1938).

the wards of the States, and in combating crime, I have had to consider most earnestly this question of temperance. It is bound up with crime, with insanity and, only too often, with poverty. It is increasingly apparent that the intemperate use of intoxicants has no place in this new mechanized civilization of ours. In our industry, in our recreation, on our highways, a drunken man is more than an objectionable companion, he is a peril to the rest of us. The hand that controls the machinery of our factories, that holds the steering wheel of our automobiles, and the brains that guide the course of finance and industry, should alike be free from the effects of over-indulgence in alcohol.

It's Not Working

But the methods adopted since the World War with the purpose of achieving a greater temperance by the forcing of Prohibition have been accompanied in most parts of the country by complete and tragic failure. I need not point out to you that general encouragement of lawlessness has resulted; that corruption, hypocrisy, crime and disorder have emerged, and that instead of restricting, we have extended the spread of intemperance. This failure has come for this very good reason: we have depended too largely upon the power of governmental action instead of recognizing that the authority of the home and that of the churches in these matters is the fundamental force on which we must build. The recent recognition of this fact by the present Administration is an amazing piece of hindsight. There are others who have had foresight. A friend showed me recently an unpublished letter of Henry Clay, written a hundred years ago. In this letter Clay said that the movement for temperance "has done great good and will continue to do more" but "it will destroy itself whenever it resorts to coercion or mixes in the politics of the country.". . .

Unexpected Consequence

This time of depression has caused us to see even more plainly than before not only the political and moral consequences of our action but its economic results as well.

We threw on the table as spoils to be gambled for by the enemies of society the revenue that our Government had theretofore received, and the underworld acquired unparalleled resources thereby. The multiplication of enforcement agencies created resentment and a cynical and complacent attitude toward lax enforcement resulting from connivance between such agencies and the law breakers. The general disregard for and defiance of such law of nationwide application bred disrespect for other law. The attempt to impose the practice of virtue by mandate of the fundamental law produced an attitude of intolerance to other forms of restraint and a denial even of the basis of authority. The violation of fundamental principles set in motion a chain of

Demobilization

After repeal of the Eighteenth Amendment, the nation celebrated in the streets, writes Fletcher Dobyns, author of The Amazing Story of Repeal. *Anti-Prohibition forces like the Association Against the Prohibition Amendment (AAPA) happily closed their doors for the last time.*

For years the members of the AAPA, their lawyers, wives, sons, "beloved authors" and other propagandists, had professed the loftiest motives. They had declared that their purpose was to stop excessive drinking and the debauching of youth, to promote true temperance, put an end to political corruption and disrespect for law, prevent the return of the saloon, and work out a constructive solution of the problem under which all profit would be taken out of the business and liquor would be sold only by the bottle in places from which every lure and enticement to drink would be absent. Repeal was celebrated by a nation-wide broadcast. Microphones were established in bars and we heard corks popping, cocktail shakers rattling, and drunken and maudlin shouts and singing from New York to San Francisco. Saloons were opened, women were admitted, barmaids and hostesses were installed and other features were added that would encourage drunkenness and vice. Three years later

consequences that no one not politically blind could fail to see; and all the time a steady flow of profits, resulting from the exactions of a newly created industry, was running into the pockets of racketeers. The only business of the country that was not helping to support the Government was in a real sense being supported by the Government. This was the business that was the direct product of the 18th Amendment and the Volstead Law—a business which is lucrative, vicious and corrupting in its influence on the enforcement agencies of Government.

Unquestionably our tax burden would not be so heavy nor the forms that it takes so objectionable if some reasonable proportion of the uncounted millions now paid to those

---

the director of the Federal Bureau of Investigation of the Department of Justice declared that "crime has reached a pinnacle of appalling height." Nearly every city in the country is now in the grip of corrupt political machines that are allied with vice and crime and sharing the profits. Not one of the lofty objectives of our noble reformers has been achieved. And yet the moment repeal was accomplished, the moment liquor was taxed and the saloons were opened, the WONPR [Women's Organization for National Prohibition Reform], the Voluntary Committee of Lawyers, and the Crusaders disbanded and closed their offices and disappeared from the scene. On December 31, 1933, the *New York Times* carried this news item:

> Washington, Dec. 30.—The Association Against the Prohibition Amendment went out of existence today. It quietly closed its offices in the National Press Building and sent its files to the Library of Congress as the record of a great adventure in sociological legislation. Having attained its objective—the repeal of national prohibition, the first amendment to the Constitution ever excised from that document—the association resisted the temptation to linger on as a "sentinel of American liberty."

Fletcher Dobyns, *The Amazing Story of Repeal.* New York: Willett, Clark, and Company, 1940.

whose business has been reared upon this stupendous blunder could be made available for the expenses of Government.

On this subject the two parties offer the voters a genuine choice this year. On the one hand a definite method of relief in the true American tradition, with the States authorized to carry out their part of the responsibility, and the Nation doing what it is practically and constitutionally able to do; on the other side, evasion and indirection.

The People Need Honesty

I should be something less than candid—in fact I should be dishonest—if I did not in this campaign continue to speak very plainly of these evasions, insincerities and deceptions. As I have repeatedly pointed out, Republican leaders are attempting to fight this battle with words. And in fighting with words we may use them either as a flaming sword, frankly, honestly and with courage, to press home the cause of truth, or we may use them as shields, to turn aside, evade and obstruct the attack of an adversary. It is in this latter sense that the Republicans have been fighting a battle of words. Now a shield is a bigger thing than a sword and so when they would use words as a defense, they must use more of them. Witness the Republican platform—long, indirect, ambiguous, insincere, false, compared with the concise sincerity of our own platform. And this is especially true of what they say about Prohibition. We first have a long, rambling party pronouncement in the Republican platform. And then we have long, rambling explanations of its meaning. Words upon words. Evasions upon evasions. Insincerity upon insincerity. . . .

The Republicans Are Split

In New York State in 1930 there was a party which tried to ride two horses at the same time. The Republican Party had one foot, its candidate for Governor, on the wet horse, and the other foot, its candidate for Lieutenant Governor, on the dry horse. The voters of New York State saw that it was a circus stunt. Honest wets and honest drys—Democratic, Republican and Independent—were disgusted. They threw the ticket into the discard.

This year the Republican national leaders have tried the same circus stunt. The answer of the voters throughout the Nation will be precisely the same.

In the last analysis, my friends, the Prohibition issue comes down to a question of faith and confidence in leadership and in the words of leaders.

However people may differ as to the principle of Prohibition, national or State, they all will agree that a temporizing and insincere policy is disastrous not only to the cause of Prohibition, but to that of temperance as well. The present leadership stands convicted of attempting to evade and confuse this issue. The honest dry will, I know, honor more the honest wet than the shifty dry; and the anti-prohibitionist prefers, I know, the four-square dry to the uncertain wet. All will join in condemning a fearful and timid practice of evasion.

Here, as before, I emphasize that the deep question in this campaign is one of confidence in leadership—in leaders. The measure of the truth of what they say is what they have said; the measure of what they will do is what they have done.

Prohibition Was a Success

George B. Cutten

President of New York's Colgate University, Dr. George B. Cutten was an outspoken man who was often criticized for his controversial views. In his book *Should Prohibition Return?* Dr. Cutten takes an unpopular stance that questions the wisdom of repealing Prohibition. When his book was published in 1944, Prohibition was a bad memory to most Americans and a stain on the records of law enforcement and government agencies nationwide. The idea of re-implementing Prohibition was not a consideration for any politician who valued his or her political career. But Dr. Cutten makes a strong case, arguing that a lack of political backing and poor enforcement undermined the successes of Prohibition. These are facts that Cutten claims were buried by the anti-prohibitionist propaganda efforts.

A mong those who are honestly endeavoring to find a solution of the problem of lessening the disastrous effects of the drinking of alcoholic beverages, there will naturally be a difference of opinion concerning the best legislative methods to be employed to accomplish the desired results. The facts show us that, so far as our experiments go in this country, undoubtedly the most effective method yet tried has been prohibition.

This statement will be met with astonishment by a great many people who have nothing else at stake than the solving of a very difficult problem. The trouble is that without doubt the most efficacious propaganda ever presented to the American people was that furnished by the advocates of repeal, largely because of the unlimited amount of money to finance it, and because it did not allow itself to be handicapped by facts.

One interesting result of this propaganda is that not only do very good and honest people believe it, but they continue to circulate some of the slogans and thereby to spread the misrepresentation. Thus you hear people who are really desirous of seeing liquor and its traffic eliminated, repeating, "You cannot make people moral by law," "Prohibition was a failure," "We must not return to the awful days of bootlegging and crime," "Prohibition brought only contempt for law," "Prohibition did not prohibit," and similar sayings, which the liquor interests are continuing to publish in a highly subsidized press.

A Time of Lawlessness

No one who would take the trouble to consult the records could have any doubt about the success of prohibition. Unfortunately, prohibition was effectively enforced in this country only two years; it is true the law was on the statute books from 1920 to 1933, but only in the first two years, 1920 and 1921, was there an adequate effort at enforcement. At the end of 1921, the liquor interests plainly saw that those entrusted with enforcement in many of the states were accepting if not encouraging a regime of perjury and anarchy—probably the greatest that this country has ever experienced.

The oaths of office of the state officials are presumedly very much the same throughout the country. The Governor of the State of New York takes the following oath: "I do solemnly swear (or affirm) that I will support the Constitution of the United States, the Constitution of the State of New York, and that I will faithfully discharge the duties of the office of governor according to the best of my ability." Notwithstanding the fact that many governors, legislators, and other officers of the states held up their hands and swore before Almighty God to uphold the Constitution of the United States, these oaths were openly violated; not only were the laws and Constitution of the United States not upheld, but the breaking of both was actually encouraged, in many cases not only by precept but by example.

Many All-Time Lows During Prohibition

Prior to the enactment of the Eighteenth Amendment, there had been two years of war-time restrictions which showed results in lessening alcoholic consumption and in the decline of the disastrous effects which follow alcoholic drinking. But in the years 1920 and 1921 there were so many all-time lows in the whole alcoholic business and in the calamitous consequences which follow in its train, that the contrast with the present situation reveals a picture which only the most prejudiced could ignore.

In those two years there were all-time lows in deaths from alcoholic poisoning, first admissions for alcoholic psychosis, crime and poverty. Jails were closed, the population of almshouses lessened, missions for drunkards were almost deserted, and other social gains revealed how successful prohibition was and could be. Before the repeal of the Amendment, children grew up to later adolescence who did not know what the word "saloon" meant, and who had never seen a drunken man. Young people who have come to maturity in the past ten years know nothing about the prohibition era, and naturally suppose that the statements repeated from repeal propaganda, and printed in liquor supported newspapers and magazines, convey a true picture of prohibition as it was. They should consult the facts. Notwithstanding the brazen and notorious dereliction of duty on the part of governors, attorneys-general, and other officers to whom the law enforcement duties of the state and nation had been assigned and entrusted, this period of effective prohibition, both in drinking and in its effects, was the low point in the history of this country.

The real purpose of prohibition is often misunderstood, sometimes deliberately. The object is not to deprive old topers [excessive drinkers] of the privilege of continuing to be pickled in alcohol. Personally, I am not at all interested in trying to convert old sinners; it is a very unprofitable project for two reasons: in the first place, it is almost impossible to convert them, and, in the second place, what you have after you get through is not worth the effort. Oh, no! The real problem is that of new recruits, and the task of preventing saloon keepers, brewers, and distillers from ensnaring the younger generation. It is a legislative method by which we propose to give less and less opportunity for the exposure of the younger people to the dangers of alcoholic indulgence.

The law was far from perfect. Any law which made it a serious crime to sell liquor, yet an occasion of boastful achievement on the part of those who bought it, certainly had its serious defects. As imperfect as it was, there was no reason for contempt for the law, but only unlimited contempt for the officials who sacrificed political and personal honor for political or personal gain by refusing to enforce it. Probably the contempt should be extended to certain citizens who desired to be called respectable, yet aided and abetted the breaking of the law by buying liquor from bootleggers to satisfy a personal craving, or to indulge a childish desire to "beat the law." The business man who met a bootlegger in his back office could have no legitimate complaint if he met a burglar in his front office, or a highwayman on his way home.

Drunkenness Is Widespread Yet Ignored

During the prohibition era it seemed as if every pint of liquor sold received front-page advertising, but now millions of gallons are not mentioned; every drunken man arrested then was the subject of comment, now hundreds of thousands, not only of drunken men but also of drunken women, receive no publicity. Then, every example of bootlegging was recited as a breakdown of law and order, but the fact that we have as much bootlegging today rarely reaches the public eye. Then, every dollar spent in enforcement was bidden a regretful adieu with sobs which could be heard around the world without the aid of radio, but now not even a whisper is uttered concerning equal or larger amounts spent for the same purpose. Then, a considerable body of women shed large, wet, salt tears because prohibition was filling our prisons, especially with those who violated the liquor laws, but today these women who wept so copiously because of the crime wave produced by prohibition are serving cocktails, dry-eyed and smiling, perfectly oblivious of the large crime wave which now exists and has existed ever since repeal.

"Prohibition does not prohibit," we are told. I suppose by that it is meant that prohibition does not annihilate the liquor traffic; unfortunately, that is true. Practically all criminal law is prohibition, and it does not annihilate crime. The Ten Commandments are practically all prohibition, so why not repeal them? We have a law prohibiting stealing, but does that annihilate stealing? If not, let us repeal it. We have a law prohibiting murder, but does that annihilate murder? If not, let us repeal it. We have a law prohibiting assault and battery, but does that annihilate assault and battery? If not, let us repeal it. Almost every time I have heard the quotation, "Prohibition does not prohibit," the quoter was a woman, and my usual high estimate of female intelligence is thereby lowered a few notches, for it is downright silly, and carried to its logical conclusion would jettison all criminal law.

It has been stated that the drys have made this a moral issue. It was not the drys who said, "You cannot make people moral by law"; and if this saying means anything at all it means that liquor drinking and liquor selling are immoral. If crime is immoral, if self-destruction is immoral, if selling others' lives and characters for one's own personal gain is immoral, then you can make people moral by law, or, at least, you can change their conduct so that they appear moral. If statistics are to be trusted at all, then prohibition did make people seem moral, at least.

A Sordid Tale

The objection to prohibition was that it was too successful; it aroused the cupidity and avarice, not only of the liquor interests, but of certain millionaire taxpayers; and joint plans were made to sacrifice human benefits and interests for individual luxuries and wealth. The story of the repeal of the Eighteenth Amendment in this country is about as sordid a tale as besmirches the pages of the history of any country at any time. By it faith in one's fellow men has been rudely shattered, and our reliance in men of big business has received a severe shock. Fortunately, only a portion of them was involved. It seems that about two hundred and fifty of this country's prominent capitalists opposed the enforcement of federal laws and openly rejoiced in the success of crime and lawlessness, coerced if they did not bribe legislators, distributed an unlimited amount of propaganda which proved to be false, and made promises which they knew they were unable to fulfill, in order to bring back a liquor business the taxes on which they thought would relieve them of their income taxes. One of them testified in a Congressional hearing that a "tax on beer would save one of my companies $10,000,000 a year." By comparison with this, Judas Iscariot, who sold his Lord for thirty pieces of silver, was a mere unsophisticated novice and Benedict Arnold was a loyal patriot.

It should not be assumed that the forces which brought about the enactment of the Eighteenth Amendment were without blame; they certainly were not, and they are surely censurable. When the amendment passed Congress, with some notable exceptions, among which was the Women's Christian Temperance Union, they took a deep breath and relaxed, fervently saying, "Well, that's finished." Had they been politicians instead of reformers, they would have known that the battle instead of being finished was only beginning, and that a battle against an unscrupulous foe, where money is involved, is never finished. Had the courage, pugnacity, determination and sacrifice been continued for twenty years after the amendment was enacted, the work would not have had to be done over again. The liquor interests, politicians, and tax dodgers created a condition in the late 1920s which it is difficult to forget, largely because the blame is incorrectly put upon the law instead of where it belongs—upon those who were willing to sacrifice their fellow men for the sake of personal gain.

Prohibitionists Moved Too Far Too Fast

From the standpoint of hindsight, the prohibition forces may well be criticized from another angle—this time in a matter of judgment. In the light of subsequent events, it seems that they went ahead too far and too fast in the promotion of a rigid national policy in some of the more populous states, especially in those states where the government of the large cities of the state, if not the state government itself, had been under the influence of criminals, and where it was certain the local law enforcement agencies would be unsympathetic and antagonistic to the enforcement of such laws. A few federal officers and courts could not possibly enforce the laws without the aid of local police agencies, and without the aid of state authorities the movement was doomed before it started.

One of the things which we would rather forget, if this were possible, but which is so completely a part of the picture of repeal that it cannot be erased, is the way people were misled by the promises of Mr. Roosevelt when he was striving to become President of the United States. While openly advocating the repeal of the Eighteenth Amendment, he connected with that certain promises on behalf of himself and the party which he represented, which led some very good people to believe that he was interested in reforming social conditions rather than in being elected—or, rather, that he was interested in being elected so that he could initiate certain reforms. Listen to some of the things he said:

> "I say to you now that from this date on the Eighteenth Amendment is doomed. When that happens, we as democrats . . . must rightly and morally prevent the return of the saloon."

In his proclamation on the repeal of the Eighteenth Amendment, Dec. 5, 1933, he further said:

> "I ask especially that no state shall by law or otherwise authorize the return of the saloon, either in its old form or in some modern guise."

"The policy of the government will be to see that the social and political evils that have existed in the pre-prohibition era shall not be revived nor permitted again to exist. . . . Failure to do this honestly and courageously will be a living reproach to us all."

There were equally strong assurances that dry territory should be protected:

"I call specific attention to the authority given by the Twenty-first Amendment to the government to prohibit transportation or importation of intoxicating liquor into any state in violation of the laws of such state."

Although Mr. Roosevelt and his associates have been in power for eleven years, so far as any person can determine they have never made the least motion to implement these promises. On the contrary, the government of which he has been not only the nominal but the actual head has accepted payment of federal liquor taxes during 1943 from 395,760 places for the sale of intoxicants, many of them as bad as, or worse than, those that preceded the days of the Eighteenth Amendment, and many of them in dry territory. Perhaps technically this acceptance of liquor revenue taxes is not a license, but, at least, it expresses acquiescence in the traffic concerned. The brewers consider it a license, at any rate. *The Brewers' Journal* of September, 1935, announced: "There are about 5500 retail establishments in Kansas for the sale of beer that have been licensed by the federal government." In 1934, Kansas had reaffirmed constitutional prohibition by 89,000 majority.

But Mr. Roosevelt was not the only president who played politics with this movement. The question of prohibition was a specific issue in the election when Mr. Hoover and Governor Smith were candidates. Mr. Hoover won. He had a clear mandate from the people to enforce the Constitution. Instead of adopting a definite policy to produce enforcement, he appointed a commission to study the question which the people had already decided. He permitted that commission to dally with their task for nearly two years, during which time divers reports and rumors were being circulated regarding their findings. When the report was released, it presented a confusion of thought on the subject which tended to undermine the confidence of the people in the administration's sincerity of purpose.

Of course, the matter goes farther back than that. President Harding made two moves which led to the sabotage of the Eighteenth Amendment before it really got started. The first was the appointment of Mr. A.W. Mellon as Secretary of the Treasury. Mr. Mellon was financially connected with distilleries, both directly and indirectly, and was entirely unsympathetic with the Amendment. His quiet and unobtrusive direction of enforcement did much to defeat it. The second blow to the amendment was to retain the matter of enforcement in the Treasury Department instead of handing it to the Attorney-General, where law enforcement belongs.

Governor Pinchot of Pennsylvania said of enforcement under President Coolidge, "As long as Coolidge talks dry and acts wet we can never have prohibition enforcement." The tradition of appointing a wet to battle the wets was carried on by the appointment of Ogden L. Mills, first as Assistant Secretary of the Treasury, and later as Secretary. Casting out demons by the prince of demons has never proved to be a success, if, indeed, it was intended to be a success.

Positions under the Volstead Act were exempted from civil service classification. That meant that all sorts of incompetent and unfit political henchmen received appointments as prohibition agents. Although Congress passed the necessary civil service legislation in 1926, no appropriations were provided to put it into effect, and not until 1930, ten years after the passage of the Volstead Act, was this desirable and necessary provision made. Of the 2500 dry agents, Major Mills estimated that three-quarters of them were of inferior type, and in 1926 General Andrews reported that 875, one-quarter of the members of his force, had been discharged for malfeasance in office.

Chronology

1874

The Woman's Christian Temperance Union is formed.

1893

The Anti-Saloon League is formed.

1900

Carry Nation begins her temperance crusade.

1917

The Eighteenth Amendment is passed by Congress; America enters World War I.

1918

World War I ends.

1919

Thirty-six states (two-thirds majority) ratify the Eighteenth Amendment.

1919

The Volstead Act is passed by Congress.

1920

The passing of the Nineteenth Amendment allows women to vote.

1920

Prohibition officially begins.

1920

Warren G. Harding is elected the twenty-ninth president of the United States.

1922

There are estimated to be five thousand speakeasies in New York alone.

1925

Al Capone takes charge of the Torrio gang in Chicago.

1926

Over 750 deaths are attributed to bad alcohol.

1928

Herbert Hoover is elected the thirtieth president of the United States.

1929

The Women's Organization for National Prohibition Reform is formed. The stock market crashes, setting off the Great Depression. It is estimated there are ten thousand speakeasies in Chicago.

1933

The Twenty-first Amendment is passed, ending Prohibition.

For Further Research

Everett S. Allen, *The Black Ships: Rumrunners of Prohibition*. Boston: Little, Brown, 1965.

Frederick Lewis Allen, *Only Yesterday: An Informal History of the Nineteen Twenties*. New York: Harper, 1931.

Charles Angoff, *The Tone of the Twenties and Other Essays*. New York: A.S. Barnes, 1996.

Edward Behr, *Prohibition: Thirteen Years That Changed America*. New York: Arcade, 1996.

Lamar T. Beman, *Selected Articles on Prohibition*. New York: H.W. Wilson, 1924.

Ella A. Boole, *Give Prohibition Its Chance*. Evanston, IL: National Woman's Christian Temperance Union, 1929.

Thomas M. Coffey, *The Long Thirst: Prohibition in America: 1920–1933*. New York: W.W. Norton, 1975.

George B. Cutten, *Should Prohibition Return?* New York: Fleming H. Revell, 1944.

Clarence Darrow, *The Story of My Life*. New York: Da Capo Press, 1996.

Fletcher Dobyns, *The Amazing Story of Repeal: An Exposé of the Power of Propaganda*. Chicago: Willett, Clark, 1940.

Editors of Time-Life Books, *The Roaring Twenties, 1920–1930*. Alexandria, VA: Time-Life Books, 1991.

Izzy Einstein, *Prohibition Agent No 1*. New York: Frederick A. Stokes, 1932.

William T. Ellis, *Billy Sunday: The Man and His Message*. Philadelphia: John C. Winston, 1914.

Ernest Gordon, *The Wrecking of the Eighteenth Amendment*. Francetown, NH: Alcohol Information Press, 1943.

Hearings Before the Subcommittee of the Committee on the Judiciary United States Senate, Sixty-Ninth Congress. Washington, DC: Government Printing Office, 1926.

K. Austin Kerr, *Organized for Prohibition: A New History of the Anti-Saloon League.* New Haven, CT: Yale University Press, 1985.

John Kobler, *Ardent Spirits: The Rise and Fall of Prohibition.* New York: G.P. Putnam's Sons, 1973.

David E. Kyvig, *Repealing National Prohibition.* Kent, OH: Kent State University Press, 2000.

Henry Lee, *How Dry We Were: Prohibition Revisited.* Englewood Cliffs, NJ: Prentice-Hall, 1963.

H.L. Mencken, *A Choice of Days: Essays from Happy Days, Newspaper Days, and Heathen Days.* New York: Alfred A. Knopf, 1980.

Charles Mertz, *The Dry Decade.* Garden City, NY: Doubleday, Doran, 1931.

Eliot Ness, *The Untouchables.* New York: Julian Messner, 1957.

Renee C. Rebman, *Prohibition.* San Diego: Lucent Books, 1999.

Ira L. Reeves, *Ol' Rum River.* Chicago: Thomas S. Rockwell, 1931.

Grace C. Root, *Women and Repeal.* New York: Harper and Brothers, 1934.

Samuel I. Rosenman, ed., *The Public Papers and Addresses of Franklin D. Roosevelt, 1928–1945.* New York: Russell and Russell, 1989.

Paul Sann, *The Lawless Decade.* New York: Crown, 1957.

Bill Severn, *The End of the Roaring Twenties: Prohibition and Repeal.* New York: Julian Messner, 1969.

Andrew Sinclair, *Prohibition: The Era of Excess.* Boston: Little, Brown, 1962.

Charles Stelzle, *Why Prohibition!* New York: George H. Doran, 1918.

Stanley Walker, *The Night Club Era.* New York: Blue Ribbon Books, 1933.

Malcolm F. Willoughby, *Rum War at Sea.* Washington, DC: United States Coast Guard, 1964.

Index